SPEAKING ILL OF THE DEAD:

Jerks in Texas History

Donna Ingham

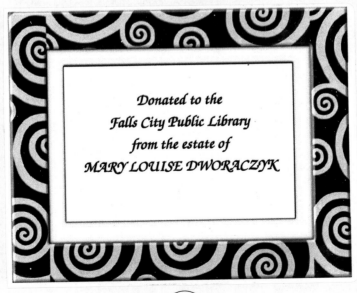

gpp

Guilford, Connecticut

To my sister, Elna, who is decidedly not a jerk

Copyright © 2012 by Morris Book Publishing, LLC

Text design by Sheryl P. Kober
Project editor: Meredith Dias
Layout: Milly Iacono

Library of Congress Cataloging-in-Publication Data

Ingham, Donna.
  Speaking ill of the dead : jerks in Texas history / Donna Ingham.
      p. cm.
  Includes bibliographical references and index.
  ISBN 978-0-7627-2706-3
  1. Texas—Biography. 2. Texas—History. I. Title. II. Title: Jerks in Texas history.
  CT262.I54 2012
  976.4—dc23
                          2011032340

Printed in the United States of America

10 9 8 7 6 5 4 3 2 1

Contents

Acknowledgments iv
Introduction v

CHAPTER 1: Jean Lafitte: Privateer Smuggler. 1

CHAPTER 2: Jim Bowie: Flawed Hero 11

CHAPTER 3: Pamelia Mann: Feisty Madam 21

CHAPTER 4: Mirabeau B. Lamar: Empire Dreamer 31

CHAPTER 5: Judge Roy Bean: Law West of the Pecos 41

CHAPTER 6: Leander McNelly: Unconventional Ranger 51

CHAPTER 7: Belle Starr: The Bandit Queen. 62

CHAPTER 8: Sam Bass: Texas Robin Hood. 72

CHAPTER 9: John Wesley Hardin: Gunslinger Lawyer 85

CHAPTER 10: O. Henry: Writer of Stories 96

CHAPTER 11: Gregorio Cortez: Man on the Run 107

CHAPTER 12: Miriam Amanda "Ma" Ferguson: First Woman
Governor of Texas. 119

CHAPTER 13: H. L. Hunt: Oil Tycoon 129

CHAPTER 14: George B. Parr: The Duke of Duval 140

CHAPTER 15: Bonnie Parker: Outlaw Partner. 151

CHAPTER 16: Madalyn Murray O'Hair: Political Activist . . . 161

CHAPTER 17: Lee Harvey Oswald: Alleged Assassin. 171

CHAPTER 18: Charles Whitman: Tower Sniper 183

Bibliography 193
Index 208
About the Author 216

Acknowledgments

To all the librarians, archivists, and photo editors who provided advice and assistance during the research process for this book, I say thanks. And to the writers—historians and biographers, for the most part—whose published research made it easier to compare different versions of the same story, I am indebted. This whole project was Globe Pequot's idea, and it has been an intriguing one from the start. It is always a pleasure to work with competent Globe Pequot editors like Meredith Rufino, Erin Turner, and Meredith Dias. They do their best to make me look good. Then there is my local support team: husband, Jerry, first reader, field research partner, and photo tracker; son and daughter-in-law, Christopher and Stephanie, 24/7 tech support; and countless other family members and friends whose interest and encouragement help keep a writer writing. Much obliged.

Introduction

At first I questioned the use of the word *jerks* in the subtitle of this book, but then I found I was hard-pressed to come up with a substitute. In its slang usage, the noun *jerk* denotes a person regarded as "cruel, rude, and small-minded" or "foolish." Some of the people detailed herein were cruel enough to take human lives; some of them were rude in manner and speech; and all could be described as small-minded at one time or another. Many of them, apparently, were very bright, but they were shortsighted and beset with a kind of tunnel vision that led them to make foolish decisions. Yes, foolish may be the most applicable adjective of all. Each of the jerks in this book behaved at one time or another "without good sense or wisdom."

More specific labels define some, but not all, of these men and women. Among these eighteen candidates for jerkdom are those who might be described by one or more of the following tags: pirate, bigamist, rogue, scoundrel, rascal, reprobate, blackguard, knave, miscreant, malefactor, varlet, fraud, con artist, crook, outlaw, swindler, cheater, charlatan, chiseler, opportunist, ne'er-do-well, cad, scalawag, rapscallion, degenerate, killer, criminal, felon, villain, assassin, or mass murderer. So, for lack of a more suitable comprehensive term, jerk will have to do.

Over half of the jerks detailed in the book were outright outlaws or other accused lawbreakers of one description or another. Jean Lafitte was a pirate, Pamelia Mann a madam, Belle Starr a horse thief, Sam Bass a train robber, John Wesley Hardin a murdering gunslinger, William Sydney Porter an embezzler, Gregorio Cortez a sheriff killer, H. L. Hunt a bigamist, Bonnie Parker a gun moll, Lee Harvey Oswald an assassin, and Charles Whitman a mass murderer. But some of the others might better be labeled as con artists or opportunists: Jim Bowie and Judge Roy Bean, most notably. Politicians who made questionable decisions included Mirabeau B. Lamar and Miriam A. Ferguson. Some merely bent existing rules or made their own: Leander H. McNelly, George Parr, and Madalyn Murray O'Hair.

As is often the case when lives are laid out side by side, in a manner of speaking, certain correspondences present themselves. For example, paths may actually cross, as in the case of Jean Lafitte and Jim Bowie, who partnered in the slave trade business at one point. In addition, both came to Texas from Louisiana, where they had been involved in questionable enterprises and where both had been on the side of the United States in the War of 1812. In Texas both were invited to join the Long Expedition, an effort to liberate Texas from both Spanish and Mexican rule, an early move toward Texas independence. Lafitte elected to remain neutral, but Bowie joined. During the time of the Texas Republic, had it not been for Mirabeau B. Lamar's intervention and presidential pardon, Pamelia Mann might have been hanged for forgery. Leander McNelly and John Wesley Hardin were involved with the Taylor-Sutton feud, on opposite sides of the law. Scripts from H. L. Hunt's *Life Line* radio broadcasts were found in Jack Ruby's coat pocket after Ruby shot and killed Lee Harvey Oswald.

Other similarities present themselves as well. Bowie was a Texas Ranger even before Texas Rangers were officially named. Later would come McNelly, Ranger captain, and Lee Hall, McNelly's successor and friend of William Sydney Porter. Hall became the prototype for Ranger characters in O. Henry's stories. Both McNelly and Porter were consumptive. Gregorio Cortez may have been the grandson of Juan N. Cortina, one of the Mexican cattle rustlers pursued by McNelly and his company of Rangers. Both Cortez and Sam Bass had ballads written about them, and both Cortez and Porter made a run for the border to escape the law. Belle Starr and Bonnie Parker elected to run with outlaws and achieved some folkloric status themselves. Parker was a poet and Porter a writer of short stories and a singer; Starr played the piano. Hardin wrote his autobiography; O'Hair kept a journal; and Whitman left notes. Parker and Ferguson may have been led astray by and were certainly influenced by the men they loved. In addition to Lafitte and Bowie, others were war heroes or at least served in the military: Lamar and McNelly during the Civil War; Cortez during the Mexican Revolution; and O'Hair, Oswald, and Whitman in more modern times. Meeting violent ends, outside of war, were Starr, Bass, Hardin, Parker, Oswald, and Whitman; Parr took his own life.

To some degree, each of the eighteen has achieved notoriety. Some made only one misstep, perhaps, in an otherwise rather admirable life. Others took a wrong turn early and stayed the path. All are fascinating studies. In a number of cases, life and legend are so intertwined that it is difficult to sort fact from fiction and separate the heroes from the goats. For that reason it may be best to approach this book as a series of narratives, bolstered by research but not intended to be definitive biographies.

For, after all, every life is a story.

JEAN LAFITTE.

Jean Lafitte: Privateer Smuggler
COURTESY OF THE ROSENBERG LIBRARY, GALVESTON, TEXAS

CHAPTER ONE

Jean Lafitte
Privateer Smuggler

In 1814 Lord Byron published a narrative poem titled "The Corsair." The closing couplet of that poem says, "He left a Corsair's name to other times, / Linked with one virtue and a thousand crimes." More than one writer since has noted a parallel between Lord Byron's protagonist and a onetime resident of Texas named Jean Lafitte.

Lafitte's one virtue, however, in any historical sense, was demonstrated the year after Lord Byron's poem was published. In January 1815, Lafitte supplied men, weapons, and his knowledge of the region to help Andrew Jackson's forces win the Battle of New Orleans in the waning years of the War of 1812. Although the British had asked for Lafitte's help in their attempt to seize New Orleans, hoping to secure a foothold in the lower Mississippi valley, he opted to fight on the side of the United States. Of course, his decision was likely based more on personal interests than on any sense of patriotism, as he hoped to gain a pardon for his illegal smuggling activities in Louisiana and get back goods confiscated by the government headed by Governor William C. C. Claiborne. Lafitte got his pardon—a presidential one from James Madison— providing he end his operation in Louisiana, but he did not get his goods back and decided to move to Texas, not then a part of the United States.

Texas was still under Spanish rule, and Lafitte's brother Pierre pledged their services to the Spanish government. They even agreed to act as spies for Spain, which was in the midst of the Mexican War of Independence. The Lafittes were quick to play politics if they could score points for themselves in the process. Jean had already proved that as he chose up sides with the

United States in its battle with England during the War of 1812. Now he and Pierre had to decide whether it was more to their advantage to side with Spain or with Mexico as Mexico sought its independence. At the moment, it seemed to be Spain. The code name for both brothers was Number Thirteen. The deal was that Pierre would keep the Spanish informed about happenings in New Orleans; Jean would do his reporting from Galveston Island, then the home base of Louis Michel Aury, who claimed to be a Mexican revolutionary.

Adding to the intrigue was a group from New Orleans said to be plotting to make Galveston a base for wresting Mexico from Spanish control. The group also planned to open a port on the Texas coast that would serve as a haven for privateers. And that's what Pierre and Jean Lafitte were, in fact: privateers, sometimes called corsairs or, most often, pirates. The Lafitte brothers preferred the privateer label, as it conveyed a certain legitimacy to what they did, attacking and looting other ships. Privateers were more or less sanctioned through letters of marque by governments in power or seeking to be in power. As it turned out, Pierre and Jean switched their allegiance from Spain to the proposed Mexican republic during Mexico's war for independence, so with Mexico's blessing, they could go after all the Spanish ships they could catch in the Gulf of Mexico. The Spanish ships, after all, were the ones with the richest cargoes. The problem was that the Lafittes' men were not always careful to check which flag was flying on captured ships, and that would soon get them in trouble with the United States again, even when they moved to Texas.

Moreover, the Lafittes first had to establish their base of operations in Texas. They did that by ousting Aury, in reality another privateer, and setting up headquarters at Galveston. It was a bloodless coup in that Jean Lafitte simply moved in while Aury was away from the island, appointed his own officers, and took command. When Aury returned several months later, he had no men left ready and willing to overthrow the interlopers, so he left, saying "the place had degenerated into a nest of pirates" and "the

[Lafitte] privateers cared little for the nationality of the vessels they met with on the sea, provided the cargo was valuable." Nest of pirates or not, the island takeover was accomplished by September 1817, and Jean Lafitte would remain the master of Galveston until early March 1821. He maintained a delicate balance in his dealings with both Spain and Mexico. Ships operating out of Galveston might fly the flag of Mexico, but they engaged in no revolutionary activities that might provoke the Spanish into invading. Lafitte chose to remain neutral when General James Long tried to recruit him to help make Texas independent from both Spain and Mexico. During the time Lafitte controlled Galveston Island, it became a center for smuggling and privateering. Jean headed up that part of the family business while Pierre continued to manage intrigues with the Spanish and Mexican governments and what business arrangements the brothers still had in New Orleans.

Jean Lafitte established a government for Galveston and a fortlike compound he called Campeche. It commanded a view of Galveston Bay and the harbor where he could anchor his fleet, and it was strategically located so that he could see any approaching ships and, if necessary, escape by one of two routes into the Gulf. His headquarters building was a two-story structure painted red. It became known, therefore, as Maison Rouge, or Red House, and was, at one time, apparently surrounded by a moat. The idea that Lafitte might even be willing to consort with the devil is perpetuated in an old legend. According to the tale, Lafitte struck a deal with Satan to build Maison Rouge in a single night with the promise that Lafitte would offer the devil the life and soul of the first creature Lafitte laid eyes on the next morning. He then arranged for a dog to be thrown into his quarters at daybreak, and that's all the devil got for his efforts. Sometimes Lafitte also conducted business aboard and lived on his ship, *The Pride*.

At first Galveston Island had very few inhabitants, except for Karankawa Indians, but within a year Lafitte's colony had grown to well over one hundred men and several women, not counting the "thousand men of mongrel breed" on ships under his command. Those "refuges from justice and victims of oppression," according to Henderson K. Yoakum, "were of all nations and languages." Reportedly, Lafitte personally interviewed all newcomers and required them to take an oath of loyalty to him. The village contained houses for the resident pirates, boardinghouses for visiting buyers, saloons, pool halls, gambling houses, a shipyard, and a large slave market. Very soon, Yoakum says, "society in Galveston, whatever may be said of its morals, began to have all the elements of permanency."

Generally said to be the more colorful of the Lafitte brothers, Jean came across as a polished gentleman and a shrewd businessman. He was said to be witty and a master of drawing room conversation. J. Frank Dobie says Jean was described "as being exceedingly handsome, even noble in appearance." Furthermore, he had "magnetism, charm, suavity, every quality necessary for one who would run innocently with the hare and at the same time bay lustily with the hounds." Although he seldom smiled, "he cultivated in a rare manner the art of being agreeable." From the start, Jean had been the one who managed the day-to-day business of outfitting privateers and arranging the smuggling of stolen goods. Pierre acted more or less as a silent partner, even though he may have been the smarter of the two. (There may have been three Lafitte brothers, but only these two are mentioned in Texas.)

Biographical details of Jean Lafitte's place and date of birth are disputed and part of the mystery of his life story. Some biographers claim he was born to wealthy parents in Bayonne or Bordeaux, France, probably in 1780 or 1781, and given a dandyish upbringing, being both pampered and well educated. Others say no, he was born as early as 1776 or as late as 1790, and they name a variety of other locations such as St. Malo, Pauillac, or Brest in France, Orduña in Spain, or Saint-Domingue (now Haiti) as possible birthplaces. One biographer even argues for Westchester, New York. By way of documentation, the 1813 registration for Pierre Lafitte's ship *Goelette la Dilidente* names Jean Lafitte as captain and lists his age as thirty-two and his birthplace as Bordeaux, France.

Using those last figures, he would have been about thirty-six when he settled in as master of Galveston and began dispatching his band of buccaneers to raid across the Gulf of Mexico and the Caribbean and stockpiling the booty they confiscated. By 1818 he was heavily into the slave trade in Texas, ten years after the United States passed a law prohibiting the importation of slaves into the United States; smuggling slaves had become a lucrative business with the invention of the cotton gin and increasing demands for cotton and for slaves to work the fields. Slavery as such was still legal in the United States, as were the buying and selling of slaves already in the country. Several loopholes in the anti-importation laws opened opportunities for Lafitte and others to capture any slave ship, regardless of its country of origin, confiscate the slaves onboard, and turn them over to a United States customs office. The slaves would not be freed, but rather sold within the United States, and half the profits would go to the people who turned them in. So Lafitte's men would target slave-carrying ships, bring the slaves to Spanish-held Texas, and sell them at discounted prices—sometimes a dollar a pound—to smugglers (including Jim Bowie). The middlemen smugglers would march the slaves to Louisiana, a part of the United States, and turn the slaves in to the custom officials. Representatives of the smugglers would then buy the slaves at the ensuing auction, and the smugglers would be rebated half the purchase price. So now the smugglers legally owned the slaves and could transport them to sell in other parts of the United States.

In spite of this new business opportunity, Lafitte and his colonists did have their troubles in 1818. Conflicts with the Karankawas resulted in deaths on both sides, and a hurricane all but inundated Galveston Island on September 12. Several people were killed, and four ships and most of the buildings—all but six—were destroyed. Furthermore, the United States government had taken notice of Lafitte's activities—especially when some of his men got greedy and attacked American ships—and seemed determined to shut down the Galveston establishment. Lafitte went so far as to hang at least one, perhaps several, of his freebooters on Pelican Island, just across the harbor from his fort, saying they were the ones responsible for the attacks on American ships. This he did, probably, as an effort to placate the authorities; then he continued his illicit activities out of Galveston.

Apparently the offenses against American traders were repeated enough times to prompt the United States, in 1821, to send Lieutenant Larry Kearney, commander of a US Navy man-of-war, to Lafitte with orders saying that Lafitte must abandon Galveston. To reinforce the demands, Kearney's ship, the *Enterprise,* anchored in Galveston harbor with its guns aimed toward Campeche. That pressure, plus the fact that Spain was rerouting its cargo-laden ships away from the Gulf because of the piracy, led to Lafitte's abandoning Galveston without a fight, although he did destroy his compound by setting fire to his fortress and settlement buildings before he left. Some say he sailed directly to Mujeres Island, off the Yucatán coast, and continued his pirating ways until his death around 1825 or 1826. Others say he first took time to bury the stockpile of Spanish gold and silver he couldn't carry away on his ships, giving rise to a great many buried treasure theories. According to legend, Lafitte himself claimed to have enough gold and silver buried on Galveston Island to build a solid-gold bridge across the Mississippi River.

Although most historians and biographers agree that Lafitte died on the Yucatán or on an island off its coast, the circumstances of his death are uncertain. Most speculate that he died of an illness, but others describe a more romantic and adventuresome departure from this life: One legend has him rescuing Napoleon from exile, burying the French national treasure somewhere near Port Isabel or Brownsville, and both of them dying in Louisiana; others suggest that Lafitte's own men killed him shortly after they left Galveston or that his entire force perished off the Yucatán in a hurricane in 1826; still another claims he changed his name and simply disappeared. The most swashbuckling account persists in legend, as Dobie describes it, saying that Lafitte "died in a daredevil engagement with a British war-sloop, his buccaneers cheering around him, his locks 'matted with blood,' the dagger in his swarthy hand streaming red." The description in *Reader's Digest*'s volume of *American Folklore and Legend* is even more detailed and graphic:

> *Above the storm of battle, Lafitte's stern voice was heard, and his red arm, streaming with gore and grasping a shattered blade, was seen in the darkest of the conflict. The blood now ran in torrents from the scuppers and dyed the waters with a crimson stain. At length, however, he fell. A ball had broken the bone of his right leg; a cutlass had penetrated his stomach.*

This version includes his last dying efforts to do in the British commander, also wounded and lying senseless near Lafitte on the deck. Lafitte "threw his clotted locks aside, and drew his hand across his brow to clear his sight of blood and mist," but he was too dizzy and weak to direct and plunge his dagger into his foe. In fact, so the story goes, "the effort to strike broke the slender thread of life and Jean Lafitte was no more."

Because fact and folklore are so mingled in biographical material about Lafitte, it is difficult to say for sure what "thousand crimes" he might have committed in comparison with Lord Byron's corsair. But there are several that recur in books and articles about Lafitte. Both a La Porte newspaper article and the Kemah Historical Society have published this tale about Lafitte's having killed a man in Charleston early in his pirating days. According the Kemah account,

> *Business brought him to Charleston Harbor; a flock of invitations brought him to a gala ball. And there he met Beatrice Toliver, a beautiful Southern Belle and daughter of a*

wealthy planter. For LaFitte it was love at first sight, and
for Beatrice it was an exciting adventure with a handsome,
daring, worldly blade of dubious reputation. Local wags
noted that LaFitte's ship dropped anchor in Charleston
more than was really necessary.

Lafitte did have competition, however, as Beatrice had "a whole gaggle of suitors." So, at another "fateful ball," one of the suitors "decided it was high time to confront LaFitte head-on. In LaFitte's presence, the young man referred to him as a 'freebooter.' It was the last word he ever said." Lafitte "swiftly and ruthlessly" killed him, after which Beatrice, "finally realizing she had been playing with fire, swore to him that she would 'never forgive' him." A "heart-broken lover," Lafitte sailed away. Mary Gertrude Ackerly labels him more "hot tempered" than heartbroken, and Dobie offers this general assessment: "When aroused, he was a desperate man indeed, and he was both an expert swordsman and an unerring shot."

Dobie says further that Lafitte "was gallant to women, but whether he was ever in love is doubtful." Nevertheless, he may have married more than once, and he is said to have had a son with a Creole mistress in Louisiana. Shortly after his arrival in Louisiana, he may have married Christina Levine and had a daughter and two sons before he was widowed. More certain is the claim that he had many "kept ladies," most of them quadroons, in his apartments in New Orleans. With one of them, Catherine Villars, he had a son, Pierre. Once in Galveston, Lafitte reportedly married Madeline Rigaud, the widow of a French settler, but she died in 1820.

Among his own men, Lafitte demanded two things: obedience and the use of the word *privateer.* Dobie recounts a story about one of Lafitte's crew members, a man named Grambo, who "hooted at the name [privateer], boldly declaring himself a pirate and calling upon his comrades to put down this genteel privateer who had come to rule over them." In response, Lafitte "pulled his pistol and shot Grambo through the heart." From that point on, Lafitte's "rule and his choice of diction were undisputed."

Before they came to Texas, the Lafitte brothers had so angered Governor Claiborne of Louisiana with their privateers' disregard for custom laws that he offered a reward for Jean's capture. It was a modest reward, generally said to be $500. Jean, who, William C. Davis says, "certainly had a taste for flair mixed with his opportunistic nature," retaliated by posting a $1,500 reward for the capture and delivery of the governor and continued to go about his business in New Orleans. Sometimes, however, threats to his domain prompted a more immediate and deadly response. In January 1814 the US Collector of Customs sent a small force to shut down the Lafitte brothers' auction of contraband goods and slaves. Lafitte's pirates killed three of the men and held the rest prisoner.

Once Lafitte arrived in Texas, Dobie says, the "record of his double dealings from the time he landed on Galveston Island until he was driven away from it would make a steel windmill giddy." As "Lord of Galveston Island" he would continue to make alliances and perpetrate betrayals as suited his needs. In 1818 he directed a French contingent up the Trinity River twenty miles or so to a remote bend near present-day Liberty, where they built a round log fort. They claimed to be refugees from war-torn Europe coming to Texas as colonists "to cultivate the vine and olive." They named their fort Champs d'Asile, "place of refuge." The Spanish were not so sure the French had come to farm, however, so they turned to Lafitte to see if there really was any planting going on. He was, after all, still Number Thirteen at that point, a spy for Spain. The leader of the French expedition was Charles Françoise Antoine Lallemand, a man some thought plotted a French invasion of Spanish Mexico, of which Texas was a part, and perhaps even a rescue of Napoleon from his second exile at St. Helena. By the spring of 1818 Lallemand had at least four hundred at the fort. Whatever Lafitte's loyalties of the moment, he apparently conspired to betray his countrymen in his guise as a Spanish spy but managed to get rid of them without their being annihilated.

According to Ed Syers, Lafitte warned Champs d'Asile of "an overwhelming Spanish army" that approached. Then he hurried to advise the "two hundred forty Spaniards struggling [through] the wilderness"—the "overwhelming army" he had described to Lallemand—that the French had fallen back to Galveston. The French were thus spared an attack by the Spanish, but the 1818 hurricane destroyed the last of their stores, and the colonists went back to Louisiana and, eventually, to Europe. They had been in Texas only nine months. The Spanish burned Champs d'Asile to the ground.

Lafitte has been described as a notorious "leader of the worst kind of fugitives, ready to turn on a commander at the slightest change of fortune." Yet even Andrew Jackson was impressed by his sophistication and found Lafitte not to be the "hellish banditti" he imagined. Dobie says Lafitte generally went unarmed, but he had "a nose that sniffed the lightest wind of adversity" and "could be depended upon to appear at the right moment provided with a brace of pistols and a 'boarding sword.'" In summary, according to Carroll A. Lewis Jr., Jean Lafitte remains an enigma in that he was "at the same time a hero and a villain, a gentleman and a cad, a patriot and a subversive. None of these qualities seemed to fit him exactly, and yet, at times he exemplified each one."

CHAPTER TWO

Jim Bowie
Flawed Hero

It may be that Jim Bowie's final rash act was his decision to ignore Sam Houston's advice. Knowing that Mexican general Santa Anna was leading a large force to San Antonio in 1836, and knowing there were not enough men to hold the Alamo in an attack, Houston had given Bowie authority to remove the artillery there and blow up the mission-turned-fort. Bowie didn't do it.

He and then-commander James C. Neill decided, first of all, that they didn't have enough oxen to move the artillery and, second of all, that they didn't really want to destroy the fortress. In support of that decision, James Bonham, one of the thirty volunteers Bowie had brought with him, organized a rally that passed a written resolution in favor of defending the Alamo. Bonham signed first, Bowie second.

Even after he learned that Santa Anna had 4,500 troops and was, in fact, headed for the city, Bowie stayed by his decision but did write letters to the provisional government asking for additional men and supplies. To the governor he stated his belief that keeping San Antonio (or Bexar, as it was called then) out of Santa Anna's possession was vital to stop the Mexican army's "march toward the Sabine [River]." So, Bowie said, "Col. Neill & Myself have come to the solemn resolution that we will rather die in these ditches than give it up to the enemy." And die Bowie did, along with an estimated 186 other Texican defenders and hundreds—perhaps over one thousand—Mexican troops, on March 6, 1836.

So yes, rash Bowie was, as had been proven before he ever got to Texas. Add to that a willingness to exploit others from time to time, and it can certainly be said that even a legitimate hero has his flaws.

Jim Bowie: Flawed Hero
COURTESY OF STATE PRESERVATION BOARD, AUSTIN, TEXAS. CHA 1989.65,
PHOTOGRAPHER: ERIC BEGGS, 2000, PRE-CONSERVATION

Although he was born in Kentucky in 1796, Bowie spent most of his life in Louisiana prior to coming to Texas in 1828. The ninth of ten children, Bowie, along with his siblings, learned to survive on the frontier. They all learned to read and write English, and Jim and his brother Rezin could also read, write, and speak Spanish and French. Jim, in particular, would use those skills to advance himself.

Early indications of Jim's willingness to do battle, whether individually or collectively, came in response to Andrew Jackson's call for volunteers to fight the British in the War of 1812. Both Jim and Rezin enlisted in the Louisiana militia in late 1814. The war ended, however, before they got to see action, and they mustered out of the military. Later Jim would answer the call from Dr. James Long to join Long's expedition bent on liberating Texas from Spanish rule. Long's attempts were ultimately thwarted, and Bowie returned to Louisiana.

Shortly before Bowie's father died in 1818 or 1819, he gave Jim and Rezin each ten slaves and some horses and cattle. The Bowie brothers teamed up and tried to develop several large estates in Lafourche Parish and Opelousas in Louisiana. They hoped to take advantage of rising land prices through speculation as Louisiana's population was growing rapidly. Since they did not have enough capital to acquire large tracts of land, they took in the pirate Jean Lafitte as a partner. Lafitte and his men were, at the time, capturing slave shipments in the Caribbean. So to raise money the Bowie brothers worked out this scheme to become de facto slave traders: The United States had, by this time, outlawed the importation of slaves but not the ownership of slaves. Anyone who informed on a slave trader smuggling in slaves would receive half of what the imported slaves would bring at auction as a reward. At least three times Jim went to Lafitte's compound on Galveston Island and bought smuggled slaves; he then returned to Louisiana, actually informed on himself, and turned the slaves over to United States customs officers who offered the slaves at auction. Bowie or his representative would buy the slaves, get half the purchase price back, and then be able to legally transport and resell the slaves at higher market value in New Orleans or somewhere farther up the Mississippi River. Jim and Rezin raised about sixty-five thousand dollars in this manner for their land speculation.

The land deals themselves soon became suspect, however, and Jim and another brother, John, found themselves involved in a major court case in the late 1820s. The United States was still trying to sort out disputed Spanish land grant claims left over from the purchase of the Louisiana Territory. In late 1827 a superior court heard 127 claims from residents who said they had purchased land in former Spanish grants from the Bowie brothers. Ultimately, research showed that the land had never belonged to the Bowies and that the original land grant documentation had been forged. Before the disgruntled purchasers could sue the Bowies, however, the documents in the case had been removed from the court, and there was no evidence on which to build a case.

On a more violent note, shortly before he left for Texas, Bowie killed a man in what has become known as the Sandbar Fight. The victim was Norris Wright, the sheriff of Rapides Parish. There was already bad blood between Bowie and Wright because Bowie had supported Wright's opponent in the sheriff's race. Wright won anyway and was a director at the bank where Bowie had applied for a loan. Wright apparently used his influence to see that the loan was refused, which, of course, angered Bowie. The two men later confronted each other in Alexandria, Louisiana, and Wright fired a shot at Bowie. Although he was uninjured, Bowie was enraged enough to attack Wright and try to kill him with his bare hands. Some of Wright's friends pulled Bowie off, but Bowie resolved after that to carry his big hunting knife with him at all times.

On September 19, 1827, about a year after the altercation in Alexandria, Bowie and Wright were both in attendance at a duel between two other men on a sandbar outside of Natchez, Mississippi. The duelists each fired two shots, and neither man was injured. So they resolved their differences with a handshake. But others on the scene, including Bowie and Wright, apparently had their own reasons for disliking each other and began fighting, with weapons in hand. In the melee Bowie was shot in the hip; he advanced on his attacker with that hunting knife, but the attacker knocked him to the ground by hitting him over the head with an empty pistol. That's when Wright got into it and fired a shot at the prone Bowie and missed. Bowie returned fire. When Wright managed to wound Bowie by running him through with a sword cane, Bowie grabbed Wright, pulled him down, and disemboweled him with a knife thrust. Wright died instantly.

Bowie's reputation for rashness and for being a superb knife fighter was fairly well cemented after that. And the fame of the Bowie knife (possibly designed by brother Rezin or by his blacksmith) spread across the country and in England as well. "Bowie knife schools" sprang up across the southwestern United States purporting to teach "the art of cut, thrust, and parry." After he recovered from his wounds, Jim Bowie decided to move to Texas. That was in 1828, and at that time, Texas was under Mexican rule. Bowie had in mind getting into land speculation again.

The problems were that, under the existing Mexican constitution, the only religion allowed was Roman Catholicism, and Mexican citizens were given preference in receiving land. Bowie was neither Catholic nor Mexican, but he moved as quickly as he could to change his status. He first got himself baptized into the Roman Catholic faith, prompted more by opportunism than conviction. Then, after traveling through Louisiana and Mississippi for eighteen months, he returned to Texas permanently and took an oath of allegiance to Mexico. He settled in San Antonio de Bexar, called simply Bexar in those days. Most of the city's inhabitants were of Mexican descent, and Bowie's fluency in Spanish stood him in good stead. He established himself in the area and became a commander of a volunteer militia assembled to keep the peace and help protect colonists from attacks by hostile Indians. It was similar to the early thirty-man ranging company founded by Stephen F. Austin, a forerunner to what would later be officially called the Texas Rangers.

Bowie was granted citizenship in 1830. Now he could buy land, up to eleven leagues. Each square league was equivalent to 4,428.4 acres. Furthermore, he convinced fourteen or fifteen other citizens to apply for land and then turn it over to him, so he soon had seven hundred thousand acres for speculation.

In 1831 Bowie got married—and lied about both his age and his net worth. His bride was nineteen-year-old Maria Ursula de Veramendi, daughter of the vice governor of the Coahuila and Texas province. Bowie was thirty-five, but he claimed to be thirty. Since it was he who was to put up a dowry, promising to pay his new bride fifteen thousand pesos (back when a peso was worth a dollar) within two years, he said his net worth was $223,000. Most of that, however, was based on his land holdings that had questionable titles. Even though the couple built a house on land near the San José Mission—land Veramendi had given them—they soon moved in with Ursula's parents, who wound up supplying them with spending money.

Perhaps itching to make a little money on his own, Bowie went looking for silver, in one way or another. Probably the most persistent legends about him, other than the ones about his role at the Alamo, have to do with his search for the so-called lost San Saba Mine. One account of his connection to the mine is tied to a story of his having heard about quantities of silver brought by Lipan Apaches to San Antonio and his determination to find the source of that silver. According to that legend, Bowie befriended the Apache chief, Xolic, gifting him with an expensive rifle, and lived among the Apaches until he was regarded as a brother. In time, so the story goes, Bowie learned the whereabouts of the Apache silver mine and abandoned the tribe to return to San Antonio. There he mounted his own expedition to mine the silver. Camped at the site of an old Spanish mission, now in ruins, Bowie and his men supposedly extracted large quantities of ore from the Apaches' mine and hauled it by burro loads to San Antonio. In this version of the tale, Bowie's treasure seeking would eventually be thwarted by attacking Indians: those Apaches whom Bowie had allegedly befriended and then betrayed. Somewhere along Calf Creek or Silver Creek in what is now Menard County, Bowie and his party had to take cover and fend off the attack, which lasted for several days. They lost one man, and the rest made it back to San Antonio.

So is there any truth to the story about the Apache silver mine and the battle on Calf Creek? Some, yes, but the rest may be a cover story. There were Apaches in the area, to be sure, and they may or may not have discovered a silver mine, but it is unlikely that Bowie ever spent time living among them. What is likely is that Bowie simply appropriated a story told by Cephas K. Ham, who had lived with the Indians, albeit Comanche, and who was a survivor of the Calf Creek Fight in Menard County, a battle that really did take place. Ham was quite a storyteller, apparently, and said he had been "adopted by the Indians and was—*almost*—shown the mine" the Comanche knew about.

It was Ham also, according to J. Frank Dobie, who perpetuated the legend that Bowie searched for the San Saba Mine. Again, perhaps giving in to the tale-teller's view that truth should never get in the way of a good story, Ham told Colonel John S. "Rip" Ford that Rezin Bowie, Jim's older brother, had already been to the mine and had even hacked off some ore with his tomahawk. But when Jim Bowie mounted an expedition to exploit the riches, Ham said, he could not find the shaft.

Adding to the confusion is an account recorded by J. W. Wilbarger in which Rezin Bowie himself alludes to a trip undertaken by the Bowie brothers and nine others in November of 1831 "from San Antonio in search of the old silver mines of the San Saba mission." It is not likely, of course, that Rezin Bowie would announce that the scouting party was, in fact, looking for a silver-laden Mexican pack train. For any silver Jim Bowie acquired came not from mining, says C. F. Eckhardt, but from bullion he took from Spanish mule trains coming up from Mexico. Caravans of up to three hundred mules would carry silver bars from Mexican mines into and sometimes all the way through Texas en route to New Orleans and other locations in the United States. They were generally guarded by fewer than a dozen men, poorly armed. The mule trains could be more than a half-mile long, so it was easy enough, in brushy country with winding trails, to hide out and then cut loose the last three or four mules without being seen. The thieves would then "head for parts unknown with nine hundred to twelve hundred pounds of bar silver."

As evidence of Bowie's propensity for gathering riches from mule trains, both Eckhardt and Robert S. Weddle cite an incident that has come to be known as the "Grass Fight," occurring shortly before the Battle of the Alamo in 1836. Perhaps thinking an approaching caravan of Mexican mules would be carrying bags of silver, Bowie led an attack on it in San Antonio. He won the battle but wound up with only bundles of hay being transported to feed Mexican army horses.

In the midst of all this alleged treasure hunting, Bowie was getting more and more involved in the politics of the province of Coahuila and Texas as tension increased between the predominantly Anglo citizenry and Mexican officials. He served as a delegate to the Convention of 1833, which formally requested that Texas become its own state within the Mexican federation. The request was not granted. That same year Bowie had a bout with malaria, or yellow fever, and a cholera epidemic threatened to strike Texas. So Bowie sent his pregnant wife and daughter with Ursula's parents to the Veramendi family estate in Monclova, but that is where the cholera in fact struck, and his whole family died. In response, he drank heavily and became "careless in his dress."

Somewhat recovered by 1834, Bowie returned to land speculation and was appointed land commissioner until May 1835 when President Antonio López de Santa Anna abolished the Coahuila y Tejas government and ordered the arrest of all Texicans, including Bowie. Joining with other Anglos agitating for war against Santa Anna, Bowie worked with William Barrett Travis, leader of the War Party, to gain support. In response to the unrest, Santa Anna began ordering large numbers of Mexican troops to Texas.

By October 1835 Bowie was acting as colonel in the volunteer militia formed by Stephen F. Austin and participated in the

Battle of Concepción in San Antonio, which ended in a stalemate. He soon resigned from Austin's army because he did not have an official commission and disliked the "minor tasks of scouting and spying." Before its final break with Mexico, Texas tried simply declaring itself an independent state within the Mexican federation and set up a provisional government. Bowie appeared before the provisional council asking for a commission in the army. The council refused the request, possibly because there was still lingering animosity about some of Bowie's past land dealings.

Sam Houston, who had assumed command of the army from Austin, offered Bowie a commission as an officer on his staff, but Bowie said no. Houston wouldn't be close enough to the action, he thought, and he wanted to be in the midst of the fighting, if fighting there would be. So he enlisted in James W. Fannin's unit as a private and participated in the siege of San Antonio de Bexar, where General Martin Perfecto de Cós, overall commander of Mexican forces in Texas, and his men were garrisoned. It was during that time that Bowie led about sixty men to intercept the Mexican burro train he believed might be carrying silver and found only grass. While he was gone, the Texicans attacked the city, and Cós surrendered and returned with his remaining troops to Mexico.

Most of the Texican volunteers believed the war was over and went home. Bowie, on the other hand, still hoping for a commission, asked the provisional council to allow him to recruit and command a regiment. Again the council turned him down since he "was not an officer of the government nor army." By this time, Texas was moving toward declaring its independence from Mexico entirely—a declaration signed on March 2, 1836—and forming its own republic, and, by this time, Houston knew Santa Anna and his forces were coming to quash the rebellion. Bowie offered to lead volunteers to defend the Alamo from expected attack. That's when Houston advised abandoning the fortress and blowing it up and when Bowie and James Neill said they would "rather die in these ditches than give [the Alamo] up to the enemy."

Neill, as it turned out, did not die. He missed the battle altogether, having gone on furlough on February 11, 1836, to visit his sick family and leaving William B. Travis, a regular army officer, in command. That rankled Bowie, who was older than Travis and had a better reputation as a soldier, or so he thought anyway. He refused to answer to Travis, so Travis called for an election allowing the men to choose their own commander. They chose Bowie, who celebrated by getting very drunk and creating havoc in San Antonio. He harassed citizens and released all the prisoners in the local jails. The disgusted Travis and a sobered-up Bowie finally worked out a compromise agreed to by the men: Travis and Bowie would command jointly, Travis leading the regular army and volunteer cavalry, Bowie the remaining volunteer companies.

Both, of course, became martyrs to the cause for Texas independence in the decisive battle on March 6, 1836. Their bodies were placed with those of the other slain Texicans on a funeral pyre and burned. Bowie's mother would say later, "I'll wager no wounds were found in his back." The actual circumstances of Bowie's death are not known, but what is known is that he was ill and likely in his room on a cot. A popular notion is that he waited, back braced against the wall, until Mexican soldiers appeared and then used his pistols and his famous knife to defend himself to the death.

One year after the battle, Juan Seguin returned to the Alamo and gathered what ashes remained from the funeral pyre and placed them in a coffin inscribed with the names of Bowie, Travis, and David Crockett. The ashes are interred at the Cathedral of San Fernando.

It's been said that "where history failed, the legends prevailed," and that is certainly the case with Bowie. Whether the course of Texas history might have been dramatically altered if he had heeded Houston's advice and walked away from the Alamo and prevented the hopeless battle the Texicans waged there, no one can know.

CHAPTER THREE

Pamelia Mann
Feisty Madam

The weather in south-central Texas was miserable in the early spring of 1836. It was rainy and cold; the roads and trails were muddy. Yet Texas colonists gathered up what few personal possessions they could carry and headed north and east under those difficult conditions. Why? Because they feared the onslaught of General Antonio López de Santa Anna and his Mexican army, especially when news reached them of the March 6 fall of the Alamo and of the massacre of James Fannin's men at Goliad three weeks later. Texas civilians, including government leaders, panicked and ran for their lives, heading for the United States border and relative safety in Louisiana or at least as far east as Nacogdoches. As more and more people heard of Santa Anna's advance and of General Sam Houston's retreat with the Texas army, the panic became universal and overwhelming. Henderson K. Yoakum, an eyewitness, records that "on every road leading eastward in Texas, were found men, women, and children, moving through the country over swollen streams and muddy roads, strewing the way with their property, crying for aid, and exposed to the fierce northers and rains of spring. The scene was distressing indeed."

Noah Smithwick, a scout ordered to Bastrop to try to get livestock across a rising river, gives an even more graphic description of what the fleeing settlers left behind:

The desolation of the country through which we passed beggars description. Houses were standing open, the beds unmade, the breakfast things still on the tables, pans of milk moulding in the dairies. There were cribs full of corn, smoke houses full of bacon, yards full of chickens that ran after us for food, nests of eggs in every fence corner, young corn and garden truck rejoicing in the rain, cattle cropping the luxuriant grass, hogs, fat and lazy, wallowing in the mud, all abandoned.

Smithwick says, "Wagons were so scarce that it was impossible to remove household goods, many of the women and children, even, had to walk."

The flight of these Texan, Tejano, and American settlers is known as the Runaway Scrape and lasted generally from the siege and fall of the Alamo until the Texans' victory at San Jacinto on April 21. Many of the refugees initially made their way to Leonard Groce's Bernardo plantation, south of present-day Navasota. Houston and his forces were there too, camped on the west bank of the Brazos River, and David G. Burnet, president of the provisional government of the newly declared republic, spent three days there with his cabinet during their retreat from Washington-on-the-Brazos to Harrisburg. Among the civilians was Pamelia Mann, who had managed to bring two large freight wagons pulled by eight oxen from her abandoned family farm. Since her husband was away during the Runaway Scrape, she was on her own, but if any woman was up to the challenge, she was.

A portrait of Mann—perhaps exaggerated at times to the point of caricature—begins to emerge from eyewitness reports about her behavior. One account, as presented by Joe Tom Davis, came from Robert Coleman, "one of Houston's unfriendly aides." Coleman claimed that Mann and Houston were soon "on very cordial terms" while camped at Groce's and alleged that when some of Houston's soldiers entered his tent unannounced, they found the general with his head in Mann's lap while she combed his hair. Stephen L. Moore continues the story with Coleman saying that Houston jumped at the sight of the men, "causing Mrs. Mann to exclaim, 'Why, General, you nearly made me put the comb into your head.'"

Certainly, whether this story is gospel truth or not, there is ample evidence that Mann was a free spirit and would not be confined to a

"woman's place" in society. She came to Texas in 1834 with her
husband, Marshall Mann, and her two sons, Flournoy (Nimrod)
Hunt and Sam Allen. The sons were fathered by her two previous
husbands, and she would marry for a fourth time to a man named
Tandy Brown before she was done. The family's arrival in Harrisburg was accomplished only after the schooner they were on out
of New Orleans had run a Mexican blockade at Galveston Island.
The Manns settled in Sterling C. Robertson's colony, and other settlers learned early on not to incur Pamelia's wrath. Davis cites an
episode recorded by a Methodist minister, O. M. Addison, in his
unpublished reminiscences. Addison recalls that his father moved
to Robertson's colony in 1835 with two ox-drawn wagons. A fence
blocked the trail, so the driver of the first wagon took it down and
drove his team through an enclosure surrounding a house. Just
as the driver of the second wagon prodded his team to follow the
first, a young man appeared, musket in hand, and told the driver
he had better turn back. Then, Addison says:

> *At this juncture, Mrs. Mann, standing in the doorway of the
> house near by, cried out to the young man in strong, angry
> tones: "Shoot him down, Nimrod! Shoot him down! Blow
> his brains out! (Nimrod was her son, Flournoy Hunt.). . . the
> young man still hesitated, when my father [having] taken
> advantage of the pause, interposed, and the matter was paci-
> fied by the wagons going around.*

This tendency to protect what was her own, by threats of violence, if necessary, would show itself again in her most famous
encounter with Sam Houston.

Mann and Houston apparently knew each other even before
they both arrived at Groce's Plantation, as Mann briefly ran an
inn at Washington-on-the-Brazos during the Convention of 1836,
where Houston and others signed the Texas Declaration of Independence on March 2. According to Moore, Houston "made his
departure [from Washington-on-the-Brazos] for the army on the

afternoon of March 6" and "mounted his trusty horse in front of Mrs. Pamelia Mann's boardinghouse." Certainly, Mann knew of Houston, at least, and so far, their relationship had been a friendly one. Maybe that is why Houston felt comfortable asking Mann for the loan of a yoke of her oxen to pull his two newly acquired six-pound cannons through the flooded, boggy countryside.

The cannons were a gift from the citizens of Cincinnati, Ohio, or at least a group of them calling themselves "Friends of Texas." On November 17, 1835, they had met in the courthouse in Cincinnati to consider giving aid to the Texas insurgents. Presiding over the meeting was Nicholas Clopper, brother-in-law to David Burnet, provisional president of the declared republic. Another "friend," Robert T. Lytle, proposed the following:

That we approve and recommend to the citizens of this meeting a plan by which the citizens of Texas shall be supplied through their agent, Mr. Smith (William Bryant) by our contributions with such an amount of hollow ware as he (Smith) may deem sufficient, to contain other provisions, by which they shall be filled, according to his judgment and sound discretion.

The resolution passed unanimously. The two cannons were manufactured, shipped down the Mississippi to New Orleans, and thence to Galveston, Harrisburg, and, finally, Groce's Plantation. They were passed through customs as "hollow ware," the customs designation for glassware and bottles. Elizabeth and Eleanor Rice, twin daughters of Dr. Charles W. Rice, a member of the Texas Navy, came to Texas aboard the same steamboat as the cannons in April 1836. Legend has it that Elizabeth and Eleanor delivered a short speech to formally present the cannons to Texas, and that is why the artillery pieces were called the "Twin Sisters" from then on. Elizabeth would write later, "I have not made much noise in this world, but my Namesake did."

Now that the Twin Sisters were part of the army, movement down the road could proceed only as fast as the cannons could be moved. "Due to the spring rains," Moore observes, "the roads were in terrible shape. Moving the cannon without oxen would be an incredible labor." Mann considered Houston's request for the loan of her oxen and agreed to it on one condition: "General," she said, "if you are going to follow the Nacogdoches road, you can have my oxen. But if you turn off and go the road to Harrisburg, you can't have them. I want them myself." Houston assured her he was "going the Nacogdoches road," but he did not say how far. The troops moved out, with the wagon master, Captain Conrad Rohrer, in charge of the oxen, mules, and horses used to transport men and equipment, including the artillery pieces. Heavy rainfall slowed their progress, but about six miles down the road they finally reached a crucial fork: a crossroads marked by what became known as the "Which-way Tree." It was the point at which Houston had to make a decision. Would he continue to retreat and take the left fork to the northeast toward Nacogdoches and maybe even cross the border into the United States for asylum? Or would he turn right—almost a right angle—down southeast toward Harrisburg and finally choose to do battle with Santa Anna? Perhaps the decision was made for him, if William C. Davis's account has merit:

> At the crossroads some [of the soldiers] began shouting "to the right boys, to the right." A group of musicians marching at the front of the column took the right turn without awaiting orders, and the rest of the army followed, including Houston, who silently rode near the back files.

At any rate, turn right they did, committed now to an inevitable confrontation some fifty-five miles away. Rohrer and his animals, including Mann's oxen, turned toward Harrisburg as well. Houston left one of his men at the crossroads "to escort and protect the families who took the left fork in their flight toward the Sabine River."

If Houston thought Mann would excuse his extended use of her property for a good cause, he was wrong. She was no Texas patriot, apparently. When she learned the fate of her oxen, she set out on the right fork road herself, on horseback, determined to catch up with the Texas army. About ten or twelve miles down the road, an irate Mann overtook Houston and his men and demanded the return of her property. The popular notion is that she arrived screaming and cursing, first confronting Rohrer. A couple of eyewitnesses said she was carrying "two pistols, a long bowie knife, and a whip." Rohrer tried to ignore her protests and urged the oxen on. She would not back off, however, much less go away, so Rohrer referred her to the general. The exchange between them went something like this: "General, you told me a damned lie. You said you was agoin' to Nacogdoches. Sir, I want my oxen." Houston replied, "Madam, don't irritate me," and went on to explain how important it was for him to have the oxen to move the cannons across the water-filled prairie. According to Joe Tom Davis, "Pamelia then unleashed a stream of oaths the likes of which Houston, himself an expert in the art of swearing, had never heard." Eyewitnesses reported that she said, "I don't give a damn for your cannon. I want my oxen." That seemed to do it, and Houston relented. "Take them, my dear woman; for God Almighty's sake, take them!" And she did.

One of the witnesses, R. H. Hunter, recorded the confrontation: "She turned a round to oxen and jumpt down with knife & cut the raw hide tug that the chane was tied with, the log chane was brokd . . ., no body said a word, she jumpt on her horse with whip in hand, & way she went in a lope with her oxen." Another eyewitness, S. F. Sparks, recalled a little more drama in the incident, saying that Mann

> drew a pistol and rode up by the side of the team and said, "Wo!" The team stopped. Houston ordered the driver to drive on. The driver fell in the water and said, "Oh, Lord, I'm shot!" The woman unhitched the oxen and drove them off.
> We called this Houston's defeat.

Only Rohrer continued to protest and wanted to go after her and try to get the oxen back: "General, we can't get along without them oxen. The cannon is done bogged down."

Houston gave his approval for the attempt but warned Rohrer, "Captain . . . that woman will fight." Rohrer replied, "Damn her fighting!" and set out on his quest while Houston asked for volunteers to help him get the cannons out of the mud and slush that came up to the men's boot tops. He was already putting his shoulder to the wheel of the cannon wagon. Hunter noted that "8 or 10 men more lade holt, out she come, & on we went." Houston said they would just have to get along as best they could. They had made it another six miles or so and set up camp before Rohrer returned empty-handed. His shirt was torn in shreds, and he said simply, "She would not let me have them." Some in camp joked that maybe "Mrs. Mann had wanted his shirt for baby rags."

In spite of this setback, Houston and his army made it to Harrisburg and on to San Jacinto. There, with the help of the Twin Sisters, they defeated Santa Anna, assuring Texas its independence from Mexico and its beginning as a republic. Returning from the Runaway Scrape, meanwhile, the Manns lived first in the Lynchburg area, where Pamelia allegedly "made free use of captured Mexicans as a labor source," and then in the vicinity of Harrisburg.

By the end of November in 1836, the capital of the republic was established in the new city named after General Houston, and in early 1837 the city had its first hotel. On the first anniversary of the Battle at San Jacinto, April 21, 1837, a catered supper at the hotel followed a celebratory ball at the Carlos Saloon. Neither establishment was finished, but both hosted Sam Houston, now president of the republic; General Thomas J. Rusk, former secretary of war; and other government dignitaries. The man who built the hotel, a veteran of San Jacinto named Benjamin Fort Smith, operated it briefly but then sold it. The buyer was Pamelia Mann, who had recently settled in Houston. As new proprietor, she named the place Mansion House, and, according to Joe Tom

Davis, she "quickly made this combination tavern and brothel the capital's leading hotel." If location is a key to success, she perhaps had an advantage in that the hotel "was located only a short distance from both the Capitol and the Executive Mansion." Archie P. McDonald says that the hotel's "clientele consisted mostly of government workers and those who had business with them."

Although it was called "commodious," the two-story hotel was small by today's standards, having only three rooms on its second floor. One of those rooms, however, was furnished like a dormitory with a number of double and single beds. The first floor had a parlor and a dining room. The parlor was fitted out with "a sofa, a cherry center table, an eight-day clock, six chairs, and a pair of spittoons." The dining room had two long tables. In addition to having their food served on china with silver cutlery, customers could order not only coffee and tea but also wine and liquor. Apparently Mann provided other amenities as well, on occasion. William Ransom Hogan says,

> *When it was desired, feminine companionship of a robust and none too virtuous nature must be provided. Boarding-houses, often dignified with the name of hotels, were set up to care for this portion of the male population which had to exist without benefit of wifely solicitude. In this last respect, Mrs. Mann and her "girls" achieved a satisfying success.*

In an attempt to rein in some of Houston's boomtown rowdiness, city officials passed morals ordinances, and within a four-year period, Mann was involved in a number of legal cases, both as a plaintiff and a defendant. She was, at one time or another, accused of larceny, assault, and fornication.

Notorious as it was for its rowdy guests, Mansion House managed to thrive. Mann earned a reputation for managing to control the brawls, duels, and police raids in the hotel. Davis says she "was known to her clientele as an expert at firearms, knives, horseback riding, and profanity and was said to have 'fought everyone except the Indians.'" Furthermore, she maintained a certain social status and had the respect of many of Houston's most prominent citizens. She could be very civic minded, turning her hotel into an infirmary of sorts during a six-month-long yellow fever and cholera outbreak at the beginning of 1838. Later that same year her son Flournoy's wedding was counted "the outstanding social event of the season." President Houston served as best man.

Still, her run-ins with the law continued. The most serious criminal charge she faced came in 1839. She was, in fact, convicted of forgery, a crime that carried a mandatory death penalty at that time. It happened this way: Mann had borrowed some money from a man named Hardy to finance her Washington-on-the-Brazos boardinghouse in 1836, soon after she came to Texas. Subsequently Hardy died, and his widow requested repayment of the loan. Mann forged a receipt showing she had already repaid four hundred dollars of the debt, and the doubting widow filed charges. Because there had been a rash of forged land titles in the new republic, the Texas Congress had passed a law making forgery a capital offense. A Harris County jury found Mann guilty, and the judge sentenced her to be "hanged by the neck till she is dead." The execution date was set for June 27. The jury that convicted her, however, recommended leniency, petitioning President Mirabeau B. Lamar. The petition took into account the severity of the punishment, saying that it was "severe and bordering on vindictive justice." Moreover, jurors recognized "the peculiar situation of the accused being a female, a mother, and a widow, and an old settler of the country." An editorial in a Houston newspaper also argued that the death penalty for forgery was too severe and that Mann should receive a lighter sentence. Lamar granted executive clemency and then a full pardon.

The next year, 1840, Pamelia Mann died on November 4, probably of yellow fever. Businesswoman that she was, she had tripled her net worth since arriving in Houston, and she left a sizable estate to her two sons. Later assessments of her included one by O. M. Addison, the man who had described her standoff with the two teamsters back in Robertson's colony. In Addison's view, Mann was forced, "perhaps from the injustice of others, to step forward in her own defense and meet lawless men on their own grounds; it was but natural that she should have developed the rude and free-spoken temper of the times and people among whom she lived." One wonders if that includes politicians.

CHAPTER FOUR

Mirabeau B. Lamar
Empire Dreamer

A large party of Comanche—warriors painted and feathered, women, and children, all dressed in their finery—rode into San Antonio on March 19, 1840. They were ready to treat for peace with the Republic of Texas, to meet in council with commissioners appointed by President Mirabeau B. Lamar. Led by Muguara (or Muk-wah-ruh, the Spirit Talker), a powerful chief, the sixty-five Comanche made up a delegation hoping to negotiate recognition of the Comancheria, their homeland, as the sovereign land of the Comanche people. They brought with them one white captive, sixteen-year-old Matilda Lockhart, and several Mexican children recently captured. With a "fair share of curiosity," twenty-two-year-old Mary Maverick and a neighbor, Mrs. Higginbotham, amused themselves by watching the procession through a picket fence.

Expecting a council of peace, a dozen chiefs and other warriors entered the Council House, a small, flat-roofed, one-story limestone building adjoining the stone jailhouse. The Comanche warriors sat on the earthen floor, as was their custom. The Texans sat on chairs on a platform facing them and offered no gifts, even though that had been customary in the past. In preliminary negotiations, Texan officials had pressured the Comanche to release all white and Mexican captives, and they first asked the Comanche where the other captives were. Lockhart had told the commissioners she had seen fifteen other prisoners at the Comanche's principal camp several days before.

Chief Muguara, as the Penateka band spokesman, said other prisoners were held by differing bands over which he had no direct control but that he was sure the captives could be ransomed in exchange for supplies, including ammunition and blankets. Failing

Mirabeau B. Lamar: Empire Dreamer
COURTESY OF STATE PRESERVATION BOARD, AUSTIN, TEXAS. CHA 1989.106,
PHOTOGRAPHER: ERIC BEGGS, 1993, POST-CONSERVATION

to understand the diffuse nature of Comanche political authority, the commissioners of the Texas government rejected Muguara's explanation. Meanwhile, the Texan militia had entered the room and taken their positions at intervals along the walls. Determining only that the Comanche would not, or could not, guarantee the return of all captives immediately, the commissioners acted on orders received from Albert Sidney Johnston, secretary of war for the republic, and approved by President Lamar: The Texans at the Council House said the chiefs would be held hostage until all the white captives were released. The Lamar-appointed interpreter did not want to deliver that message, warning that the Comanche would fight rather than be taken prisoner. Instructed to relay the warning anyway, he did so but then left the room immediately.

Sure enough, on hearing they were to be taken hostage, the Comanche drew knives, nocked arrows in bows, and attempted to fight their way out of the room. The Texan soldiers opened fire at point-blank range, killing both whites and Indians, including all twelve chiefs.

Outside the Council House, Comanche women and children heard the commotion inside and began firing their own arrows, killing at least one Texan spectator. When a small number of warriors made it out of the Council House, all the Comanche began to flee. Soldiers followed and again opened fire, killing and wounding both Comanche and Texans. Armed citizens joined the fight, shooting at all the Comanche, claiming they could not always differentiate between warriors and women and children. Maverick and the other women watching through the fence ran for the cover of their homes. Maverick was especially concerned about the safety of her young sons. She found them in the yard, protected by the Mavericks' cook, who threatened to mash in the head of a fleeing Indian with a rock if he didn't "go 'way from here." He tried but was shot down by Maverick's brother Andrew. After she had housed her little ones, Maverick looked out a door to see an Indian, "wounded and dying." A man she knew "came up just then and aimed a pistol at the Indian's head." Maverick cried out, "Oh, don't; he is dying." The big man laughed but did not fire.

According to the report filed by Colonel Hugh McLeod, written March 20, 1840, of the sixty-five members in the Comanche party, thirty-five were killed (thirty adult males, three women, and two children), twenty-nine were taken prisoner (twenty-seven women and children and two old men), and one "departed unobserved" (described as a renegade Mexican). Casualties on the Texan side numbered seven dead and ten wounded. Maverick would write in her memoirs, "What a day of horrors!"

The next day one captured Comanche woman was released and sent back to her camp to report that the other Comanche prisoners would be freed only if the remaining captives still held by the Comanche were released. They were given twelve days to comply. On April 3, after the truce deadline ended, another band of Comanche rode into town to bargain for a captive exchange, but they brought only three captives with them. One was Booker Webster, whose mother had escaped earlier with her three-year-old and arrived in San Antonio on March 26. Twelve-year-old Booker described what happened when the Comanche woman told the Penateka band about the Council House Fight and reported the Texans' demands. The Comanche were outraged at what they saw as the breaking of a truce and retaliated by torturing and killing most of their other captives, including Matilda Lockhart's six-year-old sister.

Thus ended any hope for a peaceful solution to conflicts between the Texans and the Comanche, in particular, and that was apparently just fine with Texas President Lamar. Unlike his predecessor, Sam Houston, who was the first president of the Republic, Lamar had no real desire to treat with the Indians. As an adopted Cherokee, Houston had made it his policy to negotiate treaties and territorial boundaries with the republic's various Indian tribes, including the Cherokee and the Comanche. He believed that a peaceful settlement of disputes was possible and would lead to a permanent and inexpensive solution to what Texans called "the Indian problem." Lamar insisted that the only permanent solution was to expel or kill all the Indians, and he moved quickly to implement his policy once he was elected.

Before he came to Texas, he had been associated with Governor George M. Troup, of Georgia, in driving the Creek and Cherokee from that state. He would say of Texas Indians, "As long as we continue to exhibit our mercy without showing our strength, so long will the Indians continue to bloody the tomahawk. . . . The time has come for the prosecution of an exterminating war upon their warriors, which will admit of no compromise and have no termination except in their total extinction or total expulsion."

His first step was to order Chief Bowles, a Cherokee and a friend of Houston's, to lead the Cherokee out of Texas, even though the provisional government during the Texas Revolution had made a treaty with them in 1836 granting title to their lands and acknowledging self-government to the tribes. Unfortunately, the treaty was never ratified by the Texas Senate, over which Lamar had presided as vice president of the Republic. Nevertheless, Bowles refused the order to vacate, as Lamar had suspected he would, and Lamar authorized the militia, led by General Kelsey Douglas, to use force to drive the Cherokee out of the Republic. On July 16, 1839, less than a year before the Council House Fight, the militia and a small contingent from the Texas Army attacked the main Cherokee village located on the Nueces River. Chief Bowles was among those killed, and the surviving Cherokee were forced to pack hurriedly and escape into Arkansas. They left behind homes, livestock, and crops ripening in the fields.

Pushing the limit of Lamar's policy, Douglas and his militia, by July 25, had also driven the Caddo, Kickapoo, Muskogee, Creek, Delaware, Shawnee, and Seminole tribes into Oklahoma or across the Arkansas line. Only two tribes—the Alabama and Coshatta—were permitted to remain inside the borders of the Republic. Small and inoffensive, they were nevertheless moved to less fertile lands on what was to become one of the few permanent Texas Indian reservations.

President Lamar had hoped to deal quickly with the Comanche, driving them out as he had the Cherokee and others, but the Comanche proved to be more formidable foes. The Council House tragedy provoked severe retaliatory raids by the Comanche and destroyed whatever confidence they might have had in the integrity of the Texas government. In spite of their codes and customs allowing people to wage ferocious wars against each other, the Plains Indians believed in honoring declared truces. Whites had similar codes, but, as historian T. R. Fehrenbach writes, "the Texans were not really prepared to sit down and bargain with a folk they saw as either wild beasts or cunning criminals," especially when they saw the Lockhart captive brought into San Antonio bruised and scarred and with her nose burned off to the bone. Nonetheless, the Comanche saw the Council House Fight as "the vilest treachery—the breaking of a solemn truce." To avenge the deaths of their fallen chiefs, the Comanche regrouped under Chief Buffalo Hump and waged war against the frontier settlers from West Texas all the way to the coastal towns of Victoria and Linnville in what became known as the Great Raid of 1840, taking captives and killing at least twenty-five settlers.

The Texas Rangers and militia answered by intercepting the war party on its return trip and attacking at the Battle of Plum Creek, near present-day Lockhart. The Texans engaged the Indians in a running gunfight, and eighty Comanche were reported killed. During the battle, eyewitnesses recorded atrocities on both sides. James Nichols, one of the Texans in the fight, said he saw "an old Indian squaw," seeing the Texans in full chase after the Indians, shoot and kill two of three women captives. The third she shot with an arrow as well, but it merely "inflicted a dangerous wound in [the captive's] breast." Later in the battle Nichols saw one of his fellow Texans act with a cruelty and barbarism that made him "shiver." Two men came upon a wounded, unarmed Comanche woman shot through both thighs and lying near her dead horse. Nichols had seen her and chosen to pass her by. The two men did not, and one of them drew his knife, slit her throat, and "plunged the knife to the hilt in her breast and twisted it round and round like he was grinding coffee." Nichols said he sat on his horse and wondered if there "was another man in America that claimed to be civilized that would act so cruel." Violence continued to beget violence. The Rangers claimed victory at Plum Creek, but a number of the Comanche, including Buffalo Hump, got away with many of the horses and other plunder they had taken during the Great Raid, and Buffalo Hump continued to raid white settlements for another sixteen years.

In his "recollections of old Texas days," Noah Smithwick describes a follow-up battle to the one at Plum Creek that Lamar hoped would "put a lasting quietus on the tribe." A Colonel Moore took one hundred men, including twelve Lipan Apache, "to find and rout [the Comanche] from their lair, which was located on the Red Fork of the Colorado." That expedition was counted a success as well, "the camp being burned and the occupants indiscriminately slaughtered." Smithwick says it was "the counterpart of the Indians' raid upon Victoria and Linnville," but there was no "lasting quietus," and in spite of heavy Comanche losses, "enough for vengeance still remained." As a people, the Comanche observed no peace with the Texans for nearly forty years.

So Lamar's aim "to break the predatory spirit of the Comanche and make the western frontier safe for settlement," as Charles P. Roland puts it, was far from successful, and Lamar did not drive the Comanche out of Texas. The Penateka band continued to claim territory closest to white settlement where they had been waging a continuous hit-and-run war for years with settlers along the frontier north and west of Austin, Lamar's choice as capital of the republic. Heretofore, the capital had been in Houston, but Lamar approved a commission to locate a new capital to be known as the City of Austin. According to William McCraw, it is "unquestioned" that "the influence of the 'empire dreamer' was reflected in the choice of this site." Reportedly, Lamar had earlier sat in his saddle on the hill where the capitol of Texas now stands and, viewing the charm of the scene, exclaimed to his companions, "Gentlemen, this should be the seat of a future empire."

This vision of an expansive territory for the Republic of Texas manifested itself in other ways. Indeed, as Roland observes,

Lamar, unlike Houston, "opposed annexation to the United States; instead, he dreamed of a Texas empire spreading one day to the Pacific and promised to establish at once the boundary of Texas along the Rio Grande." He claimed that annexation would mean Texas would have to surrender "the right of controlling the Indian tribes within her borders" and that the citizenry would be "alarmed for the safety of the very institution [slavery] upon which her own hopes of happiness are based." Had Lamar lived a few years longer, McCraw believes, "he would have become a militant secessionist."

It could be that Lamar's dreams of an empire reflected the general sense of destiny manifested at that time in the United States and in Texas, and the presence of the Indians in Texas offended that sense. In that regard then, as Roland surmises, Houston's "sympathy for the Indians ran counter to two of the deepest American urges, now transplanted into Texas—land hunger and the resolve to make the continent 'white man's country.'" At any rate, Lamar clearly had none of Houston's compassion for the red man, and the two leaders remained at odds. Lamar would attempt to justify his war on the Indians by branding all warriors as savages and saying, "War is itself an evil which all good people will strive to avoid; but, when it cannot be avoided, it ought to be met and pursued as will best secure a speedy and lasting peace. . . . The Indian warrior, in his heartless and sanguinary vengeance, recognizes no distinction of age, sex, or condition. All are indiscriminate victims to his cruelties. . . ."

Meanwhile, some of Lamar's constituents began to cool toward his administration for reasons other than his war on the Indians. Under Lamar's leadership, the Republic "failed to prosper"; Lamar was charged with favoritism in appointments to office, and the Republic was bankrupt. His contemporary Anson Jones wrote that "Lamar is certainly no statesman, and he and his friends are ruining the country and going to the dogs as fast as General Houston can possibly wish." Jones added, "Texas is too small for a man of such wild, visionary, vaulting ambition." In the face of such criticism, certain of Lamar's supporters thought war with the Indians would restore loyalty, so even though political expediency may not have been the cause of the administration's resolve to expel the Cherokee, "political expediency may have been a spur to action," according to Roland. Another of Lamar's contemporaries, Ashbel Smith, wrote of Lamar that he did not possess "eminent administrative ability, nor in a high degree that knowledge of human nature and tact in managing men" that might have made him a better leader.

Still, Lamar does get credit for being the "father of education in Texas." In his opening message to Congress, he said, "Cultivated mind is the guardian genius of democracy, and while guided and controlled by virtue, the noblest attribute of man." He hoped to "lay the foundation of a great moral and intellectual edifice, which will in after ages be hailed as a chief ornament and blessing of Texas." Specifically, he advocated a "suitable appropriation of lands to the purpose of general education" and thus laid the foundations of a free public school system; he sponsored legislation appropriating three leagues of land to each county for educational purposes and fifty leagues for the founding of two state colleges and universities. Perhaps this contribution accounts for his most lasting positive legacy and explains the number of public schools and the colleges and university named for him.

"By nature," says McCraw, "[Lamar] was an idealist, rather than a politician; a dreamer of empire, but without the political genius necessary to make his dreams come true." When his term as president ended in late 1841, he returned first to service in the army, and Houston became president of the Republic again. After Texas was annexed to the United States in 1845, Lamar represented Eagle Pass in the Texas State Legislature for several years, and in 1857 President James Buchanan appointed him to be the Minister to Nicaragua. He served only twenty months there before returning to Texas in 1859 because of poor health. He died of a heart attack at his Richmond plantation on December 19, 1859.

Houston, in his second term as president of the Republic, again worked to try to make peace with the Native Americans still within the borders of Texas, but he could no longer expect the Comanche, in particular, to meet in council with any degree of trust. What Mildred P. Mayhall calls the "fiasco" of the Council House meeting had "ended tragically for both sides. It was a sorry blunder, as the Texans were to learn later." Smithwick, who had earlier spent three months among the Comanche negotiating a treaty, had come to respect them as a people trying "to protect their ranging grounds." He called Muguara, the Comanche leader killed at the Council House, "my old friend," and, although Smithwick was not present, he understood why the assembled Comanche, faced with becoming hostages, reacted as they did: They, he said, "true to their character, sprang to arms, preferring certain death to the disgrace of captivity under any circumstances, and not till the last warrior—together with three women and two children—was killed, did the fight cease." In the aftermath, Smithwick says, the Comanche were "deeply exasperated at what they deemed an act of treachery."

Mayhall quotes a statement Muguara made to Smithwick during peace negotiations in 1837:

We have set up our lodges in these groves and swung our children from these boughs from time immemorial. When the game beats away from us, we pull down our lodges and move away, leaving no trace to frighten it and in a while it comes back. But the white man comes and cuts down the trees, building houses and fences and the buffaloes get frightened and leave and never come back, and the Indians are left to starve, or, if we follow the game, we trespass on the hunting ground of other tribes and war ensues.

Smithwick listened to and understood the anger and frustration of the Comanche at the continued westward expansion of the whites, but Lamar saw only savagery among a people he considered uncivilized and a hindrance to expansion.

The raids and reprisals—with atrocities on both sides—would continue in a clash of cultures that produced tragic results.

CHAPTER FIVE

Judge Roy Bean
Law West of the Pecos

"**Y**ou may have graduated at Yale or Harvard and carry a number of diplomas, but if you have not seen or heard of Judge Roy Bean of Texas, you are groping in darkness and there yet remains a large space to be filled in your classical head." So said Roy Bean himself, according to C. L. Sonnichsen, who, as Bean's biographer, was privy to some of the judge's unpublished papers. Although two of Bean's brothers made some history—Josh was the first mayor of San Diego in California, and Sam was the first sheriff of Doña Ana County in New Mexico—it is Roy who is most remembered. "Roy," says Sonnichsen, "never was more than a justice of the peace in an almost imperceptible town in West Texas, but he came closest of all to being a Great Man."

That's if notoriety counts for anything. There are enough stories about Roy Bean—some fact, some folklore—to fill a book. Several books, as it turns out. First, the facts, as far as they can be determined: Roy Bean was born about 1825 in Mason County, Kentucky. He left home at age fifteen or so, following two older brothers who had headed west. Spanish-speaking locals along their route called them *Los Frijoles*. After stops in Mexico, California, and New Mexico, Bean finally settled in Texas in the 1860s, first in San Antonio. By this time he was married and figuring out ways to support his growing family. Apparently he did this mostly by selling stolen firewood and watered-down milk from his quarters in what was already being called Beanville.

Having been a freight hauler and bartender up to this time, he signed on with the Wicks and Hickman freight line that owned most of the wooded area around his poor section of San Antonio. Part of his job was to keep an eye on the woodlots to prevent people

Judge Roy Bean: Law West of the Pecos
PRINTS AND PHOTOGRAPHS COLLECTION, THE DOLPH BRISCO CENTER FOR AMERICAN HISTORY,
THE UNIVERSITY OF TEXAS AT AUSTIN, DI 7361

from stealing the wood. But no one was keeping an eye on him. According to C. F. Eckhardt, Bean "was so enthusiastic a protector of Wicks and Hickman's property that for almost two years he held an exclusive contract with the George Holmgreen & Sons ironworks to supply their furnaces with wood." And what wood he didn't take from Wicks and Hickman, Bean poached from other people's woodlots or from wagons "confiscated" from other poachers.

In time, Bean acquired title to a shack and a couple of city lots that he agreed to swap for thirty milk cows, with the proviso that the cows be healthy and good milkers. During a "trial period," he began milking the cows and selling the milk, frequently watering it down to make it go further. One customer, a judge, complained that he found a minnow in his milk. Bean said that one of his cows must have swallowed it when she was drinking at the river. Meanwhile, Bean neglected to feed the cows. They weakened, sickened, and died, so he refused to surrender the property agreed to in the trade, saying that the cows' original owner had tried to cheat him by pawning off diseased stock.

More schemes followed. For a while Bean stole and butchered unbranded cattle and sold the meat door-to-door or from his shack that also served as saloon and store. He was clearly an opportunist who made his way with a little cunning and a lot of conning. By 1880, however, his reputation was such that most of San Antonio had grown wise and wary. He was broke and ready to move to more promising territory. His chance came when a man named T. E. "Ted" Conner and his wife simply wanted to get Bean out of Beanville, where they had established a successful store and wagon yard business. Mrs. Conner told Bean her husband would buy him out, but it was not until Mrs. Conner assured him that they would not change the name of the place to Connersville that Bean agreed to sell. A man does have his pride, after all, although Beanville didn't have much to recommend it. Sonnichsen describes it as "a poverty-stricken neighborhood, half cow pasture and half Mexican slum." Nevertheless, Mrs. Conner promised, and the deal was struck: $900 for everything he owned.

Bean, now fifty-six, invested that capital in a wagon, team, tent, several barrels of whiskey, and some firearms. Already separated from his wife, he left his children with a couple in San Antonio and set out along the route of a new railroad line being built west from San Antonio to El Paso. His idea was to have a moving saloon following the end-of-track progress along the Galveston, Harrisburg, and San Antonio Railroad line, later to be met by the Southern Pacific, which was building from the east. He set up first at the camp of Vinegaroon, named for a scorpion: "a vicious-looking creature with a stinger in its needle-like tail."

Vinegaroon was nothing more than a tent town strung irregularly along the west bank of the Pecos River and stretching for a mile or so toward the Rio Grande. Construction crews were camped there for some time as they blasted, drilled, tunneled, and graded to make way for the railroad bed. For his own campsite, Bean picked a spot near Bullis crossing just above the junction of the Pecos and the Rio Grande. Sonnichsen says, "Roy set himself up as a one-man information bureau, guide, supply officer, and friend to all who passed that way."

When the tracks moved, he followed to Eagle's Nest Camp. In the summer of 1882, Bean announced in the *San Antonio Express* that he had established a new saloon on the banks of the Rio Grande in Eagle's Nest Springs, Pecos County. "My saloon is at the meeting point of the great Southern Pacific and Western extension of the Sunset railway. No other saloon within a mile and a half from my place, and visitors will always find a quiet, orderly place, where they can get a good drink." That same summer the Texas Rangers established a "permanent camp" at Eagle's Nest as a place to bring in desperadoes. The problem was that there was no magistrate and no court in Eagle's Nest or Vinegaroon or anywhere else within two hundred miles.

The Rangers requested that a local law jurisdiction be established, and on August 2, 1882, Bean was appointed justice of the peace for the new Precinct 6 in Pecos County. His chief qualifications seemed to be that he was there and he was willing. He had only about three months of formal schooling and certainly no training in the law, although he had been a defendant himself several times in the past. In his new role he relied on a single law book, the 1879 edition of the *Revised Statutes of Texas*. If and when newer revisions were sent to him, he reportedly used them for kindling or toilet paper.

In time, the town of Eagle's Nest was permanent enough to have a post office and a new name, Langtry. Railroad records suggest that the town was named for George Langtry, the civil engineer in charge of surveying the El Paso division of the line, but Bean claimed it was he who named the town after Lillie Langtry, an English actress. Whatever the truth behind the town's naming, there is no doubt that Bean was a great admirer of the British beauty, and he named his saloon the Jersey Lilly in her honor. Born on the Isle of Jersey off the coast of England, she made several intercontinental tours acting in plays. One tour brought her to the southwestern United States in 1888, and she appeared in theaters in Galveston, Austin, Houston, Fort Worth, and San Antonio. Reports are that Bean went to see her onstage in San Antonio but was not granted an audience to actually meet her backstage. He wrote her letters inviting her to come to Langtry and appear in the opera house he had built there, but she never did. She did write him a letter expressing her regrets that she could not visit but offering to present an ornamental drinking fountain for the town square. He replied that such a gift "would be quite useless, as the only thing the citizens of Langtry did not drink was water." In her memoirs the beautiful Lillie describes making a brief stop in Langtry in January of 1904, but Bean had been dead ten months by the time she arrived. She did visit with the townspeople, who all turned out to greet her, and accepted a gift of Bean's six-shooter, a memento she is said to have hung in a place of honor in her home in England. She later wrote of Bean in her memoirs that "the stories of his ready wit and audacity made me indeed sorry that he had not lived over my visit."

When Bean first started holding court at the Jersey Lilly, there was no jail in Langtry. If the Texas Rangers required an overnight lockup, they simply chained defendants by their ankles to an old mesquite tree. Therefore most of Bean's rulings resulted in fines for those convicted, and sometimes he added an order to get out of town. Most of the persistent folklore about Judge Roy Bean describes his rather unorthodox decisions. One involved an Irishman and a Chinaman. The Irishman was the accused, a murdered Chinaman the victim. According to the oft-told tale, Bean spent hours turning the pages of the *Revised Statutes of Texas* before rapping his pistol on the bar and announcing, "Gentlemen, I find the law very explicit on murdering your fellow man, but there's nothing here about killing a Chinaman. Case dismissed." Although some would argue that this dispensation of "justice" is clearly an example of prejudice, others point out it was prompted, to some degree, in the interest of Bean's own self-preservation. Friends of the accused had supposedly threatened to destroy the

Jersey Lilly if the Irishman was found guilty. Furthermore, the Irish were good customers in the saloon; the Chinese were not.

Another tale describes Bean's methods of conducting an inquest to determine cause of death and his rulings about fining the deceased. In one version a stranger in town got drunk and fell to his death from the Myers Canyon Bridge, three miles east of Langtry. The body was brought to the Jersey Lilly, whereupon Judge Bean went through the corpse's pockets and found forty dollars and a pistol. Declaring that the man died of natural causes resulting from the accidental fall, Bean then confiscated the pistol and fined the dead man forty dollars for carrying a concealed weapon.

During the time the so-called high bridge was being built over three hundred feet above the Pecos River, a number of construction workers were killed in accidents, and Bean was frequently summoned to hold inquests. One such instance happened in 1892 when some of the top timbers of the bridge gave way and ten carpenters fell to the rocks below. Seven were killed instantly, but three barely clung to life. Judge Bean was summoned and showed up riding a mule. He looked at the ten bodies laid out in a row and said, over each, that the man had died from the fall itself and from having the timbers fall on top of him. He included the three men still breathing in his pronouncements. Someone in the coroner's jury, hastily appointed from among the bystanders, said, "Those three there ain't dead!" Sonnichsen imagines that Bean would have replied something like this: "Say, you gander-eyed galoot, who is running this here inquest? Don't you see these three fellers is bound to die? Do you think I'm damn fool enough to ride thirty miles on a sore-backed mule again to hold another inquest? Officially and legally them fellers is dead, and so I pronounce them dead, every mother's son of 'em, and you will render it as your verdict that they came to their deaths by them big timbers a-fallin' on 'em." One of the injured men lived for three days beyond his official death.

Bean served up drinks and his own brand of justice for just over twenty years, from 1882 to 1902, whether he was reelected or not. In 1886 he was voted out of office, but got himself appointed in a new precinct. Voted out again in 1896, he persisted with an unofficial compromise to try only those cases brought before him on the north side of the tracks. For all his self-serving rulings, he was probably as good a choice as could be had at that time and in that place. So say several biographers and historians who point out that a familiar saying in the 1880s was "West of the Pecos there is no law; west of El Paso, there is no God." Bean established at least some "Law West of the Pecos," prominently announced in a sign on the front of his saloon in the midst of other signs advertising ICE BEER and JUDGE ROY BEAN, NOTARY PUBLIC and, of course, THE JERSEY LILLY. He ran his courtroom efficiently, allowing neither hung juries nor appeals. Jurors were chosen from his best customers and were expected to buy a drink during each court recess. Labeling Bean "an eccentric and original interpreter of the law," Sonnichsen nevertheless says there was "a sort of common sense behind his unorthodox rulings."

In some ways Bean tried to live up to whatever reputation he had established for himself in Langtry and was even fairly respected and respectable compared to what reports came out about his earlier life. He had, for example, "shot and killed his first man, a Mexican desperado," in Chihuahua, Mexico, in 1848, according to Joe Tom Davis. Then he was arrested and jailed for attempted murder in California in 1852. With knives "beautiful admirers" smuggled to him inside a plate of tamales, he dug his way out of the jail, or so he said, although some claim he escaped through a window. Still in California, he answered the challenge to a duel from an angry suitor whose señorita he'd courted in the late 1850s and killed his opponent. Bypassing the law altogether, the dead man's friends took matters into their own hands, as reported by Richard Erdoes, and "strung him up from the nearest tree, left him dangling, and rode away." According to Bean's version of the story, he was saved from certain death by two things: One, the rope was long enough so that he could barely touch the ground with his toes and balance well enough and long enough to keep from strangling. Two, the beauty over whom the two men fought appeared with a knife and cut him down. However much Bean may have embellished that story, people who knew him recalled that his neck was so stiff that he couldn't turn his head and that he always wore a high collar or a bandana to cover a permanent scar—like maybe a rope burn—on his neck. Other skirmishes with the law in his younger days had him in court on charges of non-payment of debts, what amounted to trespass, and spousal abuse. He beat the rap every time with his own cleverness and the help of a good lawyer. Meanwhile, he picked up a sizable vocabulary of legal jargon and ideas about courtroom procedures, whether he would be entitled to perform them or not.

As justice of the peace, he performed marriages but did not have authority to grant divorces. He did anyway. He charged five dollars for weddings, ten dollars for divorces. When challenged by an assistant district attorney from Del Rio, who pointed out that Bean was granting divorces illegally and must stop, Bean replied, "I marry 'em, don't I? What I do, I certainly got a right to undo, if it ain't satisfactory." When the attorney persisted and said Bean couldn't legally "unmarry" people, Bean dismissed him with, "Maybe I can't, but I do." And he did.

In addition to simply ignoring the law, he figured ways to get around the law on occasion. In 1896 a promoter was looking for a place to stage a fight between Bob Fitzsimmons and James J. Corbet, holder of the world's heavyweight championship. Originally the fight was scheduled for Dallas, but the recently elected governor of Texas, Charles Culbertson, got busy pushing his promised reforms and called a special session of the Legislature. He proposed a law prohibiting prizefights—what he called "a public display of barbarism"—in Texas, and the legislators enacted it. What to do? The promoter turned to Mexico, just across the border in Nuevo Laredo, but the Mexican president was reluctant to disrespect Texas and the United States and forbade it. For a while it looked as if the fight venue would be moved to Arkansas, but that plan fell through as well. Meanwhile, Corbet got disgusted and announced his retirement. The promoter turned to Peter Maher, champion of Ireland, who had recently won a little-publicized bout in Nevada. He agreed to a rematch with Fitzsimmons, who had beaten him three years before.

In stepped Roy Bean. He sent a message to Dan Stuart, the fight promoter, saying, "Invite you to hold Fitzsimmons-Maher fight in Langtry. I am Law West of the Pecos and guarantee protection." On the appointed day in February, two Texas Rangers arrived with orders from the governor that the fight could not take place. Then more Rangers came. Bean moved ahead with a plan, and the sponsors brought in their own "gang of gunmen to guarantee that nobody interfered with the staging of the bout," according to William Sterling. "These pistolians were headed by former buffalo hunter and marshal of Dodge City, Bat Masterson." Bean had a crude footbridge built across the shallow Rio Grande to a sandbar on the Mexican side of the river, outside the jurisdiction of the Rangers and a two-day march from the nearest Mexican military post. The fighters entered the hastily built ring, and it took Fitzsimmons a minute and thirty-five seconds to score a knockout. The post-fight patronage at the Jersey Lilly lasted much longer, and Bean celebrated his greatest business day ever.

Always alert for opportunities to increase business, Bean kept a pet bear named either Bruno or Sarsaparilla, depending on whose account one reads, chained out on the gallery porch of the Jersey Lilly. In addition to being a general curiosity and attraction for those getting off the train in Langtry, the bear proved to be a business asset in other ways. Customers began to buy beer for the bear, and he liked it. When Bean discovered that Bruno had a taste for beer and could hold his alcohol better than most of the saloon's patrons, he encouraged strangers to bet that no man could drink more and walk straighter than the bear. Bruno's fame spread, and more strangers came to test the amazing animal for themselves. Bean sold a lot of extra beer.

Giving the man his due, it must be said, as does Ruel McDaniel, that in Bean's later years, "the greater part of his profits went to buy medicine, food, and other human necessities for the destitute

Mexicans of the section," and reports are that he always made sure the schoolhouse had free firewood in the winter. Still, his general reputation and lasting place in the folklore of Texas are summed up in brief by Loren D. Estleman: Bean, he says, was "a tricky old devil who knew how to manipulate the unique situation of his time and place and for his own benefit." Bean died, reportedly after a bout of heavy drinking, in his own bed in Langtry on March 16, 1903. He is buried at the Whitehead Memorial Museum in Del Rio.

CHAPTER SIX
Leander McNelly
Unconventional Ranger

Respected or reviled, praised or pummeled—opinions about Leander H. McNelly run to the extremes. On the one hand, he is counted a hero; on the other a villain.

His credits as a hero include his record of bravery and daring during his service in the Civil War. He enlisted in the Confederate States Army in September 1861, the year after he moved to Texas from Virginia with his family. He was seventeen. Joining Company F of the Fifth Regiment of Texas Mounted Volunteers, he soon was named aide to General Thomas Green, the commander. McNelly saw action in Texas, New Mexico, and Louisiana. In December 1863, he received a captain's commission and began leading one hundred guerrilla scouts and figuring out ingenious ways to gain information and win battles. According to Texas author Joe Tom Davis, McNelly once carried out a spying mission dressed as a woman.

Ordered to capture Brashear City, Louisiana, he managed to bluff his way to success. Reports vary about how many federal troops were stationed at Brashear City—anywhere from three hundred eighty to eight hundred, with the lower number being the one cited by contemporary Texas Ranger historians. McNelly had only his small force of fifteen to twenty scouts—or, some say, up to forty. Whatever the number, he marched his men back and forth after dark across a long bridge or in circles within hearing of the Union soldiers. As they marched, the men shouted as if they were speaking to unseen colonels and generals. At dawn, McNelly and his men rode into the Union camp under a flag of truce as if to deliver a message. They demanded unconditional surrender.

Leander McNelly: Unconventional Ranger

The bluff worked. The Union officers, believing the noise they had heard throughout the night signaled a very large force of Confederates prepared to attack, surrendered immediately. McNelly took all of the Union troops prisoner.

McNelly was wounded in battle in April 1864, but he never took sick leave or furlough in his four years of fighting, even though he had grown up sickly as a boy, suffering from consumption, or tuberculosis. In fact, one reason his family moved to Texas was the hope that its climate would improve young Leander's health. Once in Texas, McNelly worked on a sheep ranch and did regain his health, to a degree. Still, he has been described as "a tallish man of quiet manner, and with the soft voice of a timid Methodist minister"—not at all the image of a flamboyant leader of men. Later, one of his Rangers would say McNelly was only a "little runt of a feller" who looked like a "puny preacher."

McNelly's Confederate Army unit spent the last months of the war rounding up deserters and was one of the last units to disband. McNelly settled into a farm near Brenham following the war. He married Carey Cheek Matson in October 1865, and they had two children. He worked for a time in the General Land Office. But in 1870 he was recruited into law enforcement and would stay there as an increasingly controversial figure for most of the remainder of his life.

Speaking of controversial figures, Governor Edmund J. Davis, the man who recruited McNelly, is another. A Radical Republican during the post–Civil War Reconstruction days in Texas, he was elected by just over eight hundred votes as the fourteenth governor in one of the most turbulent political contests in Texas history. A number of voting irregularities were reported, including having federal troops stationed at the polls, possibly to prevent many Democrats from casting their ballots. Davis began his four-year term in 1870, and he instituted the Texas State Police in July of that year. Part of his motive, according to historian Walter Prescott Webb, was his realization "that he would need extraordinary instruments of control with which to maintain himself."

He was in no sense, Webb says, "a representative of the people of Texas," and his election "had been made possible by disfranchising the Confederates and those in sympathy with them and enfranchising their former slaves."

McNelly was one of four captains in Davis's despised State Police, later sometimes described as Davis's Gestapo. There were also eight lieutenants, two of whom were African American; twenty sergeants; and 125 privates, described as "a light and dark mixture." Ostensibly organized to combat crime statewide—and there certainly was lawlessness in the wake of the Civil War—the State Police force was neither efficient nor commendable. Joe Tom Davis says, "Citizens were soon accusing the hated State Police of killing prisoners allegedly trying to escape and of harassing voters; even some Radical Republicans thought them to be brutal and overbearing." In Webb's opinion, "The career of the state police affords a story of official murder and legalized oppression." To his credit, McNelly apparently did try to work on the side of justice during his tenure as a state policeman. The one episode generally cited about his time in service happened in February 1871. He was dispatched to arrest four men who had murdered a freedman in Walker County. McNelly made the arrests, but one man was released after a court hearing. The other three, bound over until the next term of district court, shot and wounded McNelly, with six-shooters smuggled to them by friends, as he was returning the prisoners to jail. All three got away. Governor Davis declared martial law in Walker County, and his adjutant general convened a military commission for the trial of some twenty persons said to be party to the murder and/or subsequent escape. The cost of the proceedings was paid by levying twenty-five cents per hundred-dollar-value of all taxable property in the county. McNelly criticized the move, intimating that martial law was imposed for the money it would bring.

So even though Davis's administration is credited with championing the rights of freed slaves, promoting public education, and promising protection of the frontier, Davis was defeated when he ran for reelection in 1873, and the State Police force was disbanded. On April 22, 1873, an editorial in the *Dallas Herald* said, "The people of Texas are today delivered from as infernal [an] engine of oppression as ever crushed any people beneath the heel of God's sunlight." Reconstruction in Texas came to an end, and despite what Robert M. Utley calls his "Radical Republican taint," McNelly's "wartime and police record commended him to Adjutant General [William] Steele." Steele had been appointed by the new governor, Richard Coke, to have jurisdiction over the Texas Rangers and the state militia. Coke created two branches of the Texas Rangers: a Frontier Battalion and a designated Special Force, financed by cattle ranchers who hoped the Rangers could put a stop to rampant cattle rustling. McNelly was commissioned to command the Special Force.

One of his first assignments was to muster a company of thirty men, called the Washington County Volunteers, to resolve the Sutton-Taylor feud in DeWitt County. That would be no easy task, as, by 1874, the feud "had spun completely out of control," according to Utley.

In the simplest view, the Sutton crowd represented the excesses of Reconstruction authorities and Davis's state police. On the other side was the sprawling Taylor clan, two generations and their kin by marriage, belligerently independent and unrepentantly southern. By 1874, terror, violence, killings, and lynchings, combined with stock theft, swept the county and reduced local authority to impotence.

McNelly and his men spent four months rather successfully suppressing the civil violence in the county, but at the end of that time McNelly reported that while the presence of his men had been beneficial, he was sure the fighting would flare up again as soon as the troops were withdrawn. He was right. The Sutton-Taylor feud had not yet run its course.

Nevertheless, McNelly's company was mustered out of state service on one day and mustered back in the next for a new assignment.

McNelly was commissioned to raise a new company and ordered by Steele to march at once to Corpus Christi "for service against the armed bands of Mexican marauders infesting the region between the Nueces and the Mexican Boundary." Within two days, McNelly had increased his force to forty-one men who would become very loyal to him and call themselves "Little McNellys." One of his men, N. A. Jennings, says McNelly "was well fitted for the work he had to do" and that his recruits "would not stop to count the cost beforehand, but would follow their leader with reckless enthusiasm, no matter where he might go." Once they reached the border, according to Jennings, they crossed into Mexico "for two reasons: to have fun, and to carry out a set policy of terrorizing the Mexicans at every opportunity."

It was during the eighteen months McNelly and his company were stationed in the Nueces Strip, "a hotbed of cattle thievery and banditry," that some of his methods were called into question. The area between the Nueces River and the Rio Grande, according to Webb, "stood out as something special in the way of brigandage, murder, and theft," and it had "more than its share" of outlaws such as Juan N. Cortina, Juan Flores Salinas, and John King Fisher. McNelly first sought to gather information. He paid informants who could blend in with the Mexican population on the border and alert him to impending stock raids. His other means of extracting information earned for him and his men the label *los Diablos Tejanos,* the Texas Devils. At least that is what many of the people of Mexico and the Rio Grande border region began calling the Rangers.

The fact that McNelly obtained intelligence through unorthodox methods was confirmed by Brigadier General Edward O. C. Ord, federal commander in Texas. George Durham, one of the Little McNellys, quotes a report from Ord: "Captain McNelly had a big advantage over the U.S. troops mainly because he employed means of getting information from prisoners that was denied the military. His prisoners would talk. Ours wouldn't." Those "means" included catching a suspected member of a raiding party and having him "hung up until he was made to confess where the rest of the raiders were."

McNelly did not do the actual hanging himself but left it to his chief inquisitor, a scout and guide named Jesús Sandoval, better known as "Old Casuse." Utley says that Casuse had "incurred the enmity of his countrymen across the river" because he had become "Americanized" and owned a spread fifteen miles north of Brownsville. "Efforts to kill him, burn him out, and run off his stock had driven him to the chaparral and fueled a passion for revenge against all bandits—a term he defined as loosely as did his captain."

How McNelly determined who was a bandit spy and who was not is unclear. Davis says McNelly "arrested anyone who *might be* a suspect" and then turned the prisoner over to Casuse. Casuse would slip a noose around the prisoner's neck, throw the rope over a tree limb, and hoist him off the ground repeatedly until he told the Rangers what they wanted to know. Webb interviewed a Ranger named William Callicott, one of McNelly's men, who said, "As far as we knew, this treatment always brought out the truth." But Casuse was not yet through with the prisoner. The final act, Callicott said, was "to make the bandit get on Casuse's old paint horse, and stand up in the saddle. Casuse would then make the loose end of the rope fast, get behind the horse, hit him with a hard lick and the horse would jump from under the spy, breaking his neck instantly." Ranger Durham said when he found out about these brutal executions, "it just about turned my stomach."

Two raids in particular are chronicled as evidence of McNelly's aggressive dealing with lawlessness on the Mexican border. The first occurred in June 1875 at Palo Alto, near Brownsville. It is sometimes called the "Red Raid." A group of Mexican cattle thieves, handpicked by notorious bandit gang leader Juan Nepomuceno Cortina, were driving about three hundred head of stolen cattle toward the Rio Grande when McNelly's Rangers surprised them and gave chase. The cattle were bound for Cortina's place on the Mexican side of the river and then for a steamer sailing to

Cuba. The rustlers and the Rangers fought their battle—much of it hand-to-hand—across a six-mile stretch of muddy lagoon, and it lasted almost four hours. McNelly told his troops, "Boys, across this resaca are some outlaws that claim they're bigger than the law. . . . This won't be a standoff or a dogfall. We'll either win completely, or we'll lose completely." His orders were simple and direct: "Don't shoot either to your right or left. Shoot only at the target directly in front." At the end of the day all the Mexicans were dead, as was Jack Ellis, the lone white man with them. The Rangers recovered and returned about two hundred forty head of stolen stock and lost only one man, sixteen- or seventeen-year-old L. Berry (Sonny) Smith, who forgot to heed another of McNelly's orders: "Don't walk up on a wounded man." Smith did, and the bandit killed him. The Rangers and the Fort Brown soldiers gave Smith "the biggest burial Brownsville had seen in many a day," reports Durham, and buried him with full military honors.

The bodies of the dead bandits, meanwhile, were accorded no ceremony. According to Davis, the corpses of the Cortina raiders "were stacked in the open on the town plaza [in Brownsville] and left there to draw flies, guarded and unclaimed all day. McNelly ordered this done as a grisly example to show 'how rangers deal with cow thieves.'" Utley adds that the display was intended "as a lesson for the denizens of Matamoros, who loudly vowed revenge." The Rangers did turn the bodies over to the sheriff the following day.

Tensions between the Mexicans and the Anglos, in general, were not simply of the moment. Such "ethnic animosity and cultural division" had a long history, says Utley, and "formed a backdrop for the operations of McNelly's Rangers, who shared the common Anglo attitude toward Mexicans." Just as most Mexican bandits thought killing an Anglo-Texan something to be proud of, "a considerable element" of the Anglo population along the border thought "the killing of a Mexican no crime." Utley quotes Senator Joseph E. Dwyer of San Antonio, a contemporary of McNelly's, as saying, "Americans have committed terrible outrages on citizens of Mexican origin." According to Davis, before McNelly and his troops arrived in the Nueces Strip, local citizens had formed Minute Companies to conduct counterraids against the bandits and "were hanging and killing innocent Mexicans in the area, burning their houses, and looting their ranches." McNelly ordered these vigilante groups to disband or else he would consider them outlaws, but some of his men allegedly committed similar acts.

At Palo Alto, McNelly had managed to catch the cattle thieves before they crossed the river into Mexico, but that would not be the case in what is sometimes called the Las Cuevas War near Camargo. Even the biographical entry about McNelly in the Texas Ranger Hall of Fame acknowledges that although the "Special Force" was effective, "many saw their tactics as too aggressive. For example, McNelly and his men crossed into Mexico and engaged in gun battles with bandits and citizens in attempts to recover stolen livestock. This was in contravention of U.S. policy and Mexican law and raised the ire of politicians in both countries." Specifically, McNelly had learned that the Las Cuevas Ranch in Mexico was to be the gathering point for eighteen thousand head of stolen Texas cattle. There at the Rincon de Cucharras outpost a bandit leader named Juan Flores Salinas had his stronghold. McNelly's men missed the opportunity to intercept the thieves before they crossed the Rio Grande, and McNelly decided to go after the latest rustled herd of about two hundred fifty cattle. He announced his intentions in a telegram to Austin, the state capital, saying, "I have ordered my men up and shall cross [the Rio Grande] if I can get support." To his men he said, "I can't order a single one of you men to go with me. You were hired to fight in Texas, not Mexico." He concluded by saying, "If any decide to go, step across this trail to this side." All twenty-nine present stepped across. A few hours later he sent another message: "I commenced crossing at one o'clock tonight. Have 30 men. Will try and recover cattle. The U.S. Troops have promised to cover my return."

Crossing the river by twos in a small rowboat, the men congregated on the Mexican side. McNelly remained on the Texas side "trying to line up backing for his Rangers; and the higher-ups kept saying no, on account of that would be an armed invasion of Mexico and an act of war," according to Durham. Finally, McNelly and Casuse punted across the river, and the company began to move through a heavy fog until they encountered a line camp for the main Las Cuevas. In an exchange of fire, the Rangers killed several Mexicans but lost their chance for a surprise attack on Las Cuevas itself. Durham says, "We were just watching Captain for a sign. His thinking was our thinking. We weren't twenty-nine men; we were twenty-nine McNelly shadows." The captain led the men on foot to the cover of some brush near the main ranch. With their long-range Sharps rifles, the Rangers broke up scouting attacks by the Mexicans, but McNelly called for a retreat to the river when Salinas gathered "upward of one hundred mounted men" and threatened to surround McNelly and his company. Taking cover as best they could at the river, the Rangers were still outnumbered and were running out of Sharps ammunition. They had to wait until Salinas and his men were within pistol range before they could start firing.

Fortunately for the Rangers, the US soldiers on the Texas side of the river had a Gatling gun mounted and aimed toward Mexico. A sergeant in charge swore one of the Mexicans' rifle shots landed on the Texas bank, and he thought the Mexicans were attacking his position. So "he let go with that Gatling gun and seven or eight riflemen commenced firing when the attackers got in close range." In the melee Salinas and about thirty of his men died. But McNelly still hadn't retrieved the stolen herd of cattle, and there were still Cuevians regrouping to fight.

The US military commander, Major Andrew J. Alexander, punted across the river to hand McNelly a telegram from Colonel Joseph H. Potter at Fort Brown. In it, Potter said:

Advise Captain McNelly to return at once to this side of the river. Inform him that you are directed not to support him in any way while he remains on Mexican territory. If McNelly is

attacked by Mexican forces on Mexican soil do not render him
any assistance. Let me know if McNelly acts on this advice.

"Sorry, Major, but the answer is no," McNelly said, and his men stayed put. He marched up the riverbank to the Camargo customs house and demanded that the cattle be returned. When the customs official claimed he couldn't do business on a Sunday, McNelly ferried him over to the Texas side, told him that unless the cattle were returned within the hour he would die, and waited. Durham says, "It was another one-man show by Captain." In less than an hour the herd was back in Texas, and the count was nearer four hundred than two hundred fifty.

When McNelly got around to writing a report, he said he had not been sent by the governor to write reports but "to bring law and order to a lawless country, to prove Texas was bigger than any gang or gangs of bandits." He had succeeded where other Ranger units and the military had failed. They all made lots of reports, he said, but reports weren't what bandits needed. He reasoned that "a well-placed bullet from a Sharps did more for law enforcement than a hundred reports."

As a sort of last hurrah, McNelly arrested the outlaw John King Fisher in 1876 near Carrizo without a fight and transported him to Eagle Pass, but since McNelly could produce no warrants or evidence, local authorities released Fisher. Not long after, McNelly was relieved of duty and retired to his farm near Burton. Durham says, "All of us, including Captain himself, knew he was down to be fired. His kind of law-enforcing wasn't good politics. But when they did fire him they didn't say that was the reason; the adjutant general [Steele] said it was because he was running up too many expenses with doctors and medicine." McNelly's tuberculosis had returned, and his health had greatly deteriorated. Davis sums up the general public outcry the news provoked: "After his body was used up by the state, he became a political scapegoat and was left helpless to fend for his family." McNelly died of tuberculosis on September 4, 1877.

CHAPTER SEVEN

Belle Starr
The Bandit Queen

Myra Maybelle Shirley, first called May and later Belle, moved with her parents from Missouri to Texas when she was a teenager. This would have been in 1864, during the Civil War. Belle's father, John Shirley, was first a farmer and then a successful innkeeper and stable owner in Carthage. Even though he was a Confederate sympathizer, he thought it wise to escape the violence and unrest in Missouri and move his family farther west lest they be burned out. So the Shirleys came, almost like refugees for a time, to live with Belle's brother Preston in a dugout dwelling in Scyene, about ten miles east of Dallas, and later would acquire land of their own above South Mesquite Creek. Sure enough, in September of 1864 Confederate guerrillas burned Carthage.

Belle's mother was John Shirley's third wife, Eliza Hatfield, related to the Hatfield family that feuded with the McCoys. The Shirleys, conscious of their status as a family of means, apparently wanted only the best for their only daughter and had made every effort in Missouri to give her the kind of upbringing appropriate for a proper young lady in the South.

So Belle, described as being already a superb horsewoman, always riding sidesaddle, came to Texas with "finishing school" attributes as well. She had been fairly well educated, attending Cravens, a private school, and the Carthage Female Academy. There she would have studied grammar, arithmetic, spelling, reading, Greek, Latin, Hebrew, possibly a smattering of French, needlework, and deportment. In all likelihood her father also paid extra for Belle to take music lessons. As Margaret Rau points out, "No Southern girl was considered cultured unless she could play the piano." One of her classmates recalled Belle as "a bright, intelligent girl" who

Belle Starr: The Bandit Queen
WESTERN HISTORY COLLECTIONS AT THE UNIVERSITY OF OKLAHOMA

nevertheless "was of a fierce nature and would fight anyone, boy or girl, that she quarreled with."

For all that early training toward refinement, however, perhaps it was the fierce-natured Belle who soon turned to outlaws and outlawry. Or maybe it was the company she kept. The Younger brothers—Cole, Jim, Bob, and John—and Jesse James used the Shirley home in Texas as a hideout. Outlaws all, they had ridden with William Clarke Quantrill's Raiders, a band of Southern guerrillas fighting against Union forces in Missouri, as had Belle's oldest brother, John, or Bud. Bud had been killed by pro-Union militiamen during a scouting expedition before the Shirleys left Missouri.

Some legends have it that Belle and Cole Younger were lovers and that he was the father of her first child, Rosie Lee, always called Pearl by her mother. He denied it, and Belle would never say.

In any case, certainly from the time Belle arrived in Texas, she would live as "a sexually liberated, unconventional nineteenth century woman," as Ruth Winegarten describes her. While comfortable enough in polite society and said to be an excellent conversationalist, she defied the social mores of her time. She sometimes dressed as a man or, at the other extreme, "dressed flamboyantly in black velvet, long flowing skirts, white chiffon waists, and a man's Stetson hat decorated with an ostrich plume." She sported two revolvers, pearl or ivory-handled, holstered in a cartridge belt buckled around her waist. A small woman, just over five feet tall, she was striking but not really pretty. She didn't like mirrors: "I have a face like a hatchet," she said.

Again, legends suggest that she had a fairly long string of lovers, whether or not Cole Younger was one of them, but the fact is that she seemed to be the marrying kind. She had been married to a desperado named Jim Reed for two years when Pearl was born. They too had known each other in Missouri and married in Collin County in 1866. Pearl was born in 1868.

Reed didn't care much for farm life, apparently, growing restless and spending much of his time gambling, racing horses, and making trips to Indian Territory. When his brother was killed in Arkansas, Reed went after the man who shot him. Reed tracked down the alleged murderer and killed him, so now Reed was a wanted man himself. He gathered up his family—Belle and little Pearl—and headed west, all the way to California. There Belle gave birth to a son in 1871. She named him James Edwin. All was well until Reed got arrested for passing counterfeit money and the police discovered he was wanted for murder. Reed jumped bail and headed back to Texas. Belle and the children followed by stagecoach.

By now Belle's father was successful enough to provide the Reeds with a small farm of their own to work, but they turned it into a hideout for horse thieves instead. Meanwhile, Reed still had a price on his head and thought he might be safer in Indian Territory. Belle went with him, leaving the children with her parents in Scyene. In the fall of 1873, Reed and some cronies robbed a rich farmer named Watt Grayson and escaped with thirty thousand dollars in gold. Some reports were that one of the gang was a woman dressed like a man and presumed to be Belle, but there is no reliable documentation that she was a participant in the robbery. Lawmen stepped up their search for Reed in particular, and while he went into hiding, Belle returned once more to live with her parents in Texas. She may well have spent time in Dallas hotels as well, having a good time spending some of Reed's stolen money.

Even as a man on the run, Reed continued to add to his crimes. In April of 1874, back in Texas again, he and his gang held up the Austin–San Antonio stage, robbing the passengers and looting the mail sacks. A large reward was posted for the gang's capture, whereupon a lawman named John T. Morris got on Reed's trail and tracked him to Paris, Texas. There Morris shot and killed Reed and collected the reward. And Belle was left a widow.

In the years following Reed's death, Belle worked her farm and welcomed outlaws passing through. After her father's death in 1876, she sold the farm, moved to Dallas, sent Pearl to acting school, and shipped her son, Ed, off to live with Reed relatives in

Missouri. In a letter to Reed's family, she commented on Pearl's budding theatrical career: "She has been playing on the stage here in the Dallas theatre and gained a world-wide reputation for her prize performance." That may have been a mother's pride showing, but Belle's motives seemed to be focused on providing Pearl with a means of being an independent woman: "My people were very opposed to it [Pearl's work in the theater] but I wanted her to be able to make a living on her own, without depending on anyone."

Belle soon took up with menfolk again. For a while it was a Kansas miner named Bruce Younger, an old family friend and uncle to the Younger brothers. Richard and Judy Dockery Young claim she married him in 1878 in Kansas "and then abandoned him at their apparent mutual consent." Then it was Sam Starr, a tall, handsome Cherokee nine years younger than Belle. In 1880 they married in a tribal wedding and moved to acreage on Indian land on the Canadian River in what is now Oklahoma. Belle told a newspaper reporter, "There, far from society, I hoped to pass the remainder of my life in peace and quietude."

But she didn't. Most of the Starrs' friends were outlaws, after all, and once again, Belle's home became a hideout, the only entrance to it via a canyon so narrow a wagon could barely pass through. In notes Belle gave a *Dallas Morning News* correspondent in 1886, she recalled that Jesse James was among the first guests, one of "the boys who were friends" of hers "from times past." She called them her "old associates," and her reputation as "a woman of some notoriety from Texas" grew. She complained about the "slanderous tongues" of her neighbors, "a low down class of shoddy whites," and maintained, "In all the world there is no woman more peaceably inclined than I."

Nevertheless, while they were holed up at the Starr place, the outlaws continued to steal horses, rob salesmen, and sell moonshine to the Indians. Belle was apparently satisfied to be almost solely in the company of men and live her life in some degree of isolation. She said in a newspaper interview, "So long had I been estranged from the society of women, whom I thoroughly detest, that I thought I would find it irksome to live in their midst. So I selected a place that but few had ever had the gratification of gossiping around." Winegarten says Belle seemed to enjoy "the free camaraderie of male society," complaining once that "all women discuss are pumpkins and babies." She may or may not have sat in on the outlaws' planning meetings, but she very likely was in on the buying and selling of stolen horses.

It was the horse dealings that brought a US marshal to arrest both Sam and Belle. A man named Andrew Pleasant Crane claimed they had stolen his horse, and that was a federal offense. They were jailed in Fort Smith, Arkansas, where they stood trial and were found guilty. Judge Isaac Parker, called "the hanging judge" for having sent eighty-eight men to the gallows, passed sentence on them, letting them off with one-year sentences in a Michigan prison. Sam was put to hard labor, breaking up rocks with a sledgehammer, but Belle had an easier time of it. Described as being a model prisoner, she caught the eye of the prison warden, who had her work in his office and let her teach music to his children. She even did some writing in her spare time. Both Starrs served only nine months of their sentences and then returned to their home on the Canadian River. Belle's jail time added to her reputation as a notorious outlaw, and, as John Q. Anderson observes, Eastern newspapers had begun to call her "The Queen of the Bandits," "The Lady Desperado," "Wild Woman of the West," and "The Petticoat Terror of the Plains."

Stories from those who actually met her, however, suggest that she was regarded as more of a curiosity than a terror. Anderson recounts a tale told to him by his father, who once saw Belle interrupt her biscuit making in camp to give a shooting exhibition. Some of the men in camp had been target shooting and got into an argument about who was the best shot. "I'll show you who can shoot," Belle said. Then "she drew both of her pearl-handled sixshooters and methodically, hand over hand, emptied them into the knot in the tree. The argument was over." Biographer Glenn Shirley agrees that she was an "expert horsewoman and a deadly shot with pistol or rifle." Yet there is no evidence that she ever killed anyone or even participated in bank, train, or stagecoach robberies or in cattle rustling.

Horses may have been a different matter. In 1886 she was again charged with horse theft, but this time she provided adequate legal defense to get herself acquitted. Meanwhile, Sam and an Indian policeman got into a shoot-out at a dance and killed each other. A widow once more, Belle wasted little time finding a new lover, Jim July, also called Bill July or Jim Starr. Legends say that she had July change his name to Starr, but biographers explain that Tom Starr, Sam's father and Belle's former father-in-law, adopted July and gave him the Starr name. Belle and Jim, who was fifteen years her junior, married and continued to live in Indian Territory. Carl Green and William Sanford say that at this point Belle "turned over a new leaf" and "let everyone know that outlaws were no longer welcome at Younger's Bend" there on the Canadian River.

Her reformation, if such it was, did not bring her peace. Perhaps trying in earnest to rid Younger's Bend of the outlaw element—excepting her husband, an alleged horse thief—she quarreled with Edgar Watson, a neighbor to whom she had rented land. She had found out that Watson was wanted for murder and threatened to turn him in to authorities. Some say it was Watson who ambushed her near Eufala, Oklahoma, as she rode home on February 3, 1889, just two days before her forty-first birthday. At any rate some assailant knocked her from her horse with a shotgun blast and left her to die on a muddy road. Another possible suspect was her own son, Ed, with whom she frequently argued. She had recently given him a beating for mistreating her horse. No one was ever convicted.

Belle was buried on her place on the Canadian River, where her daughter later erected a headstone engraved with a bell, a star, and a likeness of Belle's favorite horse, Venus. The inscription on the stone reads "Shed not for her the bitter tear, / Nor give the heart to vain regret. / 'Tis but the casket that lies here, / The gem that filled it sparkles yet."

After Belle's death, the legends about her spread beyond Dallas, the Cherokee Nation, and parts of Arkansas, where she had spent most of her life. The *New York Times,* in a February 6, 1889, obituary news item, labeled her "the most desperate woman that ever figured on the borders." The publisher of the *National Police Gazette,* Richard K. Fox, published *Bella Starr, the Bandit Queen, or the Female Jesse James* in 1889, the same year she died. It sold for a quarter and was but loosely based on her real life, describing her as being "more amorous than Anthony's mistress, more relentless than Pharoah's daughter, and braver than Joan of Arc." Nowadays various websites, perhaps drawing from sources like Fox's publication, have perpetuated some of the more exaggerated or romantic aspects of Belle's story and claim, without qualification, that she was the "most well-known lady bandit in American history," that she was "a horse thief, bootlegger, cattle thief, [and] suspected robber of stagecoaches," and that she could be called "a lady Robin Hood—stealing from the rich and giving to the poor." She has been popularized in as many as fifty books; in a long-running 1939 Broadway play, *Missouri Legend;* and in two Hollywood movies, both titled *Belle Starr.* In 1941 Gene Tierney played the title role, and in 1980 Elizabeth Montgomery starred in a made-for-television film. In 1969 Betty Grable starred in a London musical, and an off-Broadway play, *Jesse and the Bandit Queen,* had a successful run in 1975. In some of the tales about her, Belle has become something of a folk heroine.

These later accounts often sensationalize Belle's love life, crediting her with not only her four marriages but also with a string of lovers, starting with Cole Younger and continuing through other outlaws with names like Jack Spaniard, Jim French, John Middleton, and Bluford "Blue" Duck. She did have a studio photograph made with the last named, Blue Duck, but there is an explanation offered for that. He was a Cherokee Indian indicted for murdering a farmhand. She agreed to be photographed with him—he being seated and handcuffed, she standing beside him—at the request of his attorney. According to Richard D. Arnott, the attorney "apparently thought it would help his client in his pending appeal of a death sentence." This was "the first and last time Belle saw Blue Duck."

Mixed in with the legends about her sometimes scandalous behavior are tales attesting to her view of herself as the lady her mother and father wanted her to be. Corinne Naden and Rose Blue cite a couple of examples: In addition to riding sidesaddle, the feminine way, she didn't smoke cigars, as some western women did, and "she could get downright difficult about being treated correctly." They pass on a story about Belle's hat blowing off when she was riding. "She asked a man, also on horseback, to retrieve it. He didn't. Instantly, she whipped out her gun and pointed it between his eyes. He jumped off his horse for the hat. Belle said, 'The next time a *lady* asks you to pick up her hat, do as she tells you.'"

In summarizing her life for a *Fort Smith Elevator* reporter in 1888, about a year before her death, she said, "I regard myself as a woman who has seen much of life." That could certainly qualify as understatement. She had lived through the Civil War, reportedly acting as a spy while still a teenager in Missouri, gathering information at social gatherings about positions of Union troops and passing that information on to the Confederates. She consorted with Confederate guerrillas, including her brother Bud, and then spent the rest of her years in the company of outlaws who were frequently on the run. She was once quoted by a Dallas newspaper reporter as saying, "I am a friend to any brave and gallant outlaw, but have no use for that sneaking, coward class of thieves who can be found in every locality, and who would betray a friend or comrade for the sake of their own gain. There are three or four jolly, good fellows on the dodge now in my section, and when they come to my home they are welcome, for they are my friends, and would lay down their lives in my defense at any time the occasion demanded it, and go their full length to serve me in any way."

It is unlikely that the facts of Belle Starr's life will ever be entirely distinguishable from the fiction, given the level of notoriety she reached, especially after her death. There are very few primary sources from which to draw information, but there are at least some responsible journalists and biographers who have attempted to determine the facts about her life and death that belie the exaggerated rumors about her. They also frequently recognize the paradox that she was. Margaret Rau, for example, says, "Although Belle delighted in excitement and the company of outlaws, she was also intensely proud of her old and respected family name and fiercely guarded its reputation." Rau calls Belle "one of America's early feminists, who vigorously defended her right to equality as a woman in a male-dominated world," and Ruth Winegarten describes her as "the most remarkable woman in the history of border outlawry." Belle's choices, nevertheless, did not necessarily bring her long-term happiness or success or glamour. As early as 1910, Oklahoma newspaperman Frederick S. Barde concluded that "those who knew her well see no glamour in what she did—she was merely a dissolute woman, unfortunate in her early life, and in her later years merely a companion of thieves and outlaws."

CHAPTER EIGHT
Sam Bass
Texas Robin Hood

Four men reached the outskirts of Round Rock, Texas, on the afternoon of July 19, 1878. It was a Friday. They intended to scout the area before they robbed a bank there the next day. The leader of the gang was Sam Bass, a young man who had come to Texas from Indiana, by way of Mississippi, in 1869 or 1870. Settling first in Denton County, he spent most of his time there engaged in horse racing, but he seemed an industrious enough fellow. With boyish good looks, he was companionable, yet said to be sometimes sober and serious. Those who knew him said he could neither read nor write and that he thought and talked slowly. Who could have guessed that he would be sung into immortality as the Texas Robin Hood? Yet Walter Prescott Webb says Bass "was perhaps the first Yankee to gain popularity in Texas after the Civil War."

The 1910 edition of John Lomax's *Cowboy Songs and Other Frontier Ballads* includes "The Ballad of Sam Bass," an anonymously written biographical narrative with a dozen stanzas. It begins:

Sam Bass was born in Indiana, it was his native home,
And at the age of seventeen young Sam began to roam.
Sam first came out to Texas a cowboy for to be—
A kinder-hearted fellow you seldom ever see.

According to J. Frank Dobie, Bass "never was much of a cowboy," but William Edward Syers argues that "he was a good cowboy." Historians and biographers are often at odds about the details when it comes to Bass's life and legend. By some accounts, while in Denton, Bass was briefly a deputy sheriff until he quit or his horse racing and gambling got him fired; others say he did

Sam Bass: Texas Robin Hood
PRINTS AND PHOTOGRAPHS COLLECTION, THE DOLPH BRISCO CENTER FOR
AMERICAN HISTORY, THE UNIVERSITY OF TEXAS AT AUSTIN, DI 7362

work for the sheriff, but only as a janitor, a farmhand, or a teamster. He's also said to have tried digging for gold, driving a mule train, and running a store. For certain he would later turn to robbing stagecoaches, trains, and banks and become "noted for his openhanded generosity with the money he obtained at gun point." That's when the legends about him began.

He was always pretty free with his money, apparently, as his ballad continues with these lines:

> *Sam used to deal in race-stock, one called the Denton mare;*
> *He matched her in scrub races and took her to the fair.*
> *Sam used to coin the money, and spent it just as free;*
> *He always drank good whiskey wherever he might be.*

The Denton mare was a little sorrel. She may not have been "the speediest thing in Texas," according to Webb, but "she was fast enough to carry Sam into the sporting world." One story describes Bass's winning a herd of Indian ponies in a match race beyond Fort Sill in Indian Territory. The owner of the ponies refused to hand them over, so Bass, under cover of darkness, collected them anyway and maybe a few extras to boot.

A good money manager Bass was not. He partnered with Joel Collins in the summer of 1875 in San Antonio on a cattle deal. They bought a small herd on credit, drove the cattle up the trail to Dodge City, Kansas, shipped them on to Nebraska, drove them farther to Dakota Territory, and reportedly sold them for eight thousand dollars cash. Rather than paying off their loan, they invested their cattle money in wagons and teams and did some freighting in the area until winter set in. Then, according to Webb, "they sold their teams and opened a pleasure resort devoted to liquor, cards, and dissolute women." Dobie's research too suggests that they "spent all the money in riotous living."

> *Sam left the Collins ranch in the merry month of May,*
> *With a herd of Texas cattle the Black Hills for to see;*

Sold out in Custer City, and then got on a spree—
A harder set of cowboys you seldom ever see.

That's when Sam turned to a life of crime, first robbing stage-coaches that connected the Black Hills with the outside world. That did not turn out to be very profitable.

Then in September 1877 he and Collins and four other men robbed a Union Pacific express train in Nebraska. It was carrying California gold, and they each got away with ten thousand dollars in newly minted twenty-dollar gold pieces.

On their way back to Texas they robbed the U. P. train,
And then split up in couples and started out again;
Joe Collins and his partner were overtaken soon,
With all their hard-earned money they had to meet their doom.

Kansas lawmen and US soldiers caught up with Collins and his runaway partner, Bill Heffridge, and killed them, recovering twenty thousand dollars of the loot. But Sam escaped and "made it back to Texas, all right side up with care; / Rode into town of Denton with all his friends to share." In the months following the train robbery, Sam's "reputation for lighthearted generosity began to grow into legend." So says Dobie. "Now he had something to be generous with—something that did not belong to him."

Sam's ballad claims only "three robberies did he do; / he robbed all the passenger, mail, and express cars too." In truth, there were many more than three robberies following that successful one in Nebraska, but most of the succeeding ones, now back in north Texas, paid poorly. Still, people said Bass would often tip the porters and the brakemen. Since he rarely robbed people individually, preferring to take from the trains mail sacks full of money going to or coming from corporations, the general public saw him as a somewhat romantic figure, and the people were generally for him. The Texas Rangers, on the other hand, were decidedly against him, and the railroad and express companies were offering healthy rewards for his capture. Even though four train robberies, all near Dallas, between late February and early April in 1878 netted him and his gang little more than pocket change, they nevertheless "aroused corporate and political Texas as no other crimes had," according to Robert M. Utley. Bass was "on the dodge" and covering lots of country. Since it was dangerous for him or his men to show their faces in a town and buy provisions, they simply took what they needed from time to time—but not without paying, so the stories go.

A farmer named Hoffman noticed one morning that some shelled corn was missing from his crib. Obviously someone had come in the night and stolen a fair-size sackful. But the sack must have had a hole in it because Hoffman could trail grains of the corn that had fallen on the ground as the culprit beat his retreat back to a campsite. As Hoffman neared the campsite, he realized it was occupied by the Bass gang and turned back home. A few days later Bass saw Hoffman, apparently recognized him, and handed him a twenty-dollar gold piece. "I had to have some corn in a hurry the other night," Bass said.

Another tale says a neighbor paid Denton County resident Shelton Story a dollar to deliver a hindquarter of beef to some men camped at a certain spot on the Denton Creek bottom. Story was to ask no questions. He tied the meat, wrapped in an old slicker, behind his brand-new saddle—the first new saddle he had ever owned. About the middle of the afternoon Story found the campsite, noting that there were four men, "all wearing six-shooters." The spokesman for the group said, "Well, get down, kid, and stay awhile." Although he had no desire to stay awhile, Story got down and untied the slicker-wrapped package of beef. The man said, "That's sure a fine saddle you're riding." Story agreed. "Kid, how about trading your saddle for mine?" Story looked at the man's old saddle. It was a wreck, all but falling apart; only the saddlebags were any good. But with all that firepower around there seemed to be little choice. And by now, the man had identified himself: "I'm Sam Bass." So Story made the trade, feeling as if he "had been taken advantage of by the meanest, low-downest man in Texas."

When he got home, Story yanked the old saddle off and threw it on the ground. He heard the chink of metal. Investigating, he found three twenty-dollar gold pieces in one saddlebag and three more in the other saddlebag—enough to buy an even better saddle than the one he had traded; plus he could add a "silver-plated bit and spurs, Navajo blanket, fancy boots, leggings, everything." His opinion of "the meanest, low-downest man in Texas" no doubt changed.

Even youngsters stored up stories about encounters with the magnanimous outlaw. A man named Jackson, who grew up in Denton County, told Dobie about the time he and his little brother were each carrying a bucket of water from the well to their house. Bass and his gang rode up to them. "Give us a drink, kids," Bass said. The boys, proud to be in the company of such a famous man, happily ladled out the water with a gourd. Bass noticed that Jackson's little brother was all crippled up with rheumatism. Maybe that prompted Bass to be a little more generous than usual when paying for his water. He pitched the boys four silver dollars.

As a result of what C. F. Eckhardt calls Bass's "free distribution of double eagles in his flush times," the outlaw had a number of "accomplices" who helped him escape capture. In fact, some of them "took a perverse delight in waiting until Sam's dust settled on the northbound trail and then pointing the pursuers east." Dobie collected a story from a grandmother who said when she was a young woman she had a dressmaker's shop. One day Bass was in town buying ammunition when he saw a sheriff approaching. Bass dodged into the woman's shop, and she recognized him. She told him to get under a mountain of ruffles she had on the floor—trimming she had piled up to use on party dresses. Bass did. The sheriff came in the shop, looked around, and left. The dressmaker told her story for years afterward, always ending it by saying, "Lots of folks loved Sam."

Even those who set out on their own or with posses to try to capture Bass for the reward money offered could be won over. A settler named Hide, in Stephens County, was one such bounty hunter. He told about the time he was going to the store in Caddo to enlist another man or two to ride with him in search of the outlaw. As Hide dismounted with all his artillery, a man leaving the store with a sack of provisions asked him where he was going. "I'm going to hunt down Sam Bass," Hide answered. "Then you don't need to go any farther," the stranger said. "You've found him." Bass then asked Hide how many children he had and went back in the store to buy a dozen apples, a sack of candy, and some coffee. "Take the candy and apples home to your children," he said. "When you get there, make yourself a big pot of coffee and never tell a soul you have seen Sam Bass." Hide did not tell a soul until thirty years later.

The makeup of Bass's gang stayed fairly small, although, as Utley puts it, the gang was one "of shifting numbers and composition." The ballad says,

Sam had four companions—four bold and daring lads—
They were Richardson, Jackson, Joe Collins, and Old Dad;
Four more bold and daring cowboys the Rangers never knew,
They whipped the Texas Rangers and ran the boys in blue.

Collins, of course, died in the wake of the Union Pacific holdup. It's not clear who Richardson was, but Old Dad was probably John Underwood. Frank Jackson would be with Bass to the end.

Sam and another companion, called Arkansas for short,
Was shot by a Texas Ranger by the name of Thomas Floyd;
Oh, Tom is a big six-footer and thinks he's mighty fly,
But I can tell you his racket—he's a deadbeat on the sly.

Arkansas Johnson lay dead by the tracks after one of the gang's hits on the Texas and Pacific near Dallas. Webb tallies as many as nine members in the train-robbing gangs, and Eckhardt says there may have been as many as twenty-three at any one time.

The composer of the ballad does not give much credit to the Texas Rangers and "the boys in blue," that is, militia men who were on the Bass gang's trail, but the lawmen began a serious manhunt in the spring of 1878. Major John B. Jones organized a detachment of Texas Rangers in north Texas and offered the command to Junius "June" Peak, a former deputy sheriff and city marshal. Peak and a few of his Rangers caught up with Bass on Salt Creek in Wise County, and in the shoot-out one of Bass's men was killed. Two others were captured, but Bass, Seaborn Barnes, and Frank Jackson escaped and made it through the elm thickets back to Denton County. One of the captured outlaws was Jim Murphy.

> *Jim Murphy was arrested, and then released on bail;*
> *He jumped his bond at Tyler and then took the train to Terrell;*
> *But Major Jones had posted Jim and that was all a stall,*
> *'Twas only a plan to capture Sam before the coming fall.*

In exchange for his freedom, Murphy agreed to a deal with the Rangers, promising to rejoin Bass's gang and betray the outlaw leader.

Following the Rangers' orders, Murphy posted bond and then failed to show up in court when it convened in Tyler. The word was out that he had "jumped bail" by the time he found the Bass gang in the Denton County elm bottoms and said he wanted to rejoin. Bass and Barnes were suspicious, but Jackson, who was Murphy's cousin, vouched for him and said the other two would have to kill Jackson before they could kill Murphy. Bass relented but reminded Murphy "how freely he had handed out his gold to Murphy's family" and that any betrayal would be "a low-down, mean, and ungrateful trick." Bass and Barnes continued to watch Murphy carefully as the gang planned one more robbery to get some traveling money before they headed to Mexico. This time they set their sights on a bank and began to scout for a likely one to rob. They stopped in Ennis, Temple, Waco, and Belton but ruled each one out for one reason or another. While in Belton they sold an extra pony there to buy feed for their horses, and while the others were distracted during the horse transaction, Murphy finally got his chance to write a quick note to alert the Rangers that it had been decided: The gang had chosen a target.

"We are on our way to Round Rock to rob the bank. For God's sake be there to stop it." Murphy gave the note to a man who promised to deliver it to the Rangers.

With Major Jones when he got and read the note were three men: Dick Ware, Chris Conner, and George Harrell. Jones dispatched those three to Round Rock immediately, saying he would follow the next day. Jones rode the train, accompanied by Travis County deputy sheriff and former Ranger Maurice B. Moore. Once in Round Rock, Jones recruited two more ex-Rangers, a stable keeper named Henry Highsmith and Williamson County deputy sheriff A. W. Grimes. Additional Rangers arrived from Austin and Lampasas. Jones scattered the men around town. According to James B. Gillett, one of the Rangers en route to Round Rock when the shoot-out took place, "Jones advised Grimes to keep a sharp lookout for strangers, but on no account to attempt an arrest until the Rangers could arrive." That is advice Grimes should have taken.

Murphy managed to tarry in a feed store at the edge of town when Bass, Barnes, and Jackson rode into Round Rock about 4 p.m. on July 19, 1878. The three tied their horses in an alley and walked up the street to buy some tobacco at Copprell's, a clapboard general store right next to the bank. They also intended to do some last-minute reconnaissance before their planned robbery the next day. They knew the bank would be open until five o'clock on Saturday for Town Day, the day when farmers, ranchers, and cowboys would be coming in to do business and make deposits. Some of Jones's men saw the strangers but apparently did not recognize them. Moore, however, noticed a bulge that indicated at least one of the men had a pistol. Moore told Grimes, whose job it was to enforce an ordinance that everyone had to check his arms while in town. Grimes and Moore followed the men in the store, and Grimes said to Bass, "I believe you have a pistol." Bass replied, "Yes, of course I have a pistol." At that all three robbers pulled their guns and started firing, killing Grimes as he backed toward the door. Moore returned fire, wounding Bass in the hand, before staggering himself with a bullet in his lung. He would survive. The outlaws burst from the store and out into the street, headed for their horses.

Ranger Ware was all lathered up ready to get a shave in a nearby barbershop when he heard the gunfire. He rushed into the street and advanced toward the fleeing bandits. They fired at him, one of their bullets hitting a hitching post so close to his head that it sent splinters into his face. By this time the other lawmen had converged on the scene, as had a number of armed citizens. In the ensuing firefight Ware took aim and shot Barnes in the head and killed him. A coroner's jury later gave Harrell credit for wounding Bass, saying the ball from Harrell's pistol first struck Bass's cartridge belt, cutting two cartridges and entering Bass's back just above the right hip bone. The bullet tore Bass's "right kidney all to pieces," according to Gillett. Jackson held the Rangers off long enough to unhitch Bass's horse and help Bass into the saddle. Then Jackson mounted his own horse, and off the two men galloped, Jackson still helping steady Bass as they rode. And where was Murphy, the betrayer? Standing in the doorway of May's store, watching the escapees ride by at a dead run. Posses of Rangers and civilians followed in pursuit.

Bass and Jackson left the road and hid in the woods. Weak as he was from loss of blood, Bass could go no farther. He told Jackson to go on without him. Jackson protested. "No, Frank," Bass said, "I am done for." When night fell, the pursuing posses gave up the hunt but resumed their search early the next morning. Meanwhile, Bass had managed to crawl to a nearby house asking for water; then he crawled back into a thicket and propped himself up against the trunk of a live oak tree. That's where the Rangers found him. As they approached, Bass called out, "Don't shoot. I am the man you are looking for. I am Sam Bass." Ware would say in an interview later:

I found the dying outlaw and put his head in my lap and gave him water from a small puddle I had scooped from the brim of my hat. He said he was dying, that he was from Indiana, but made me promise I would go back there and console his mother. Later I did go and found his mother, but never told her of Sam's robberies and life of crime. . . .

The Rangers took Bass to Round Rock, called in a doctor and nurse to tend to his wounds, and tried to interrogate him. To the last, he would not betray his friends. He said it was against his principles to "blow on my pals." He lingered through that Saturday and died on Sunday, July 21, 1878, his twenty-seventh birthday. He was buried in the old Round Rock cemetery. His sister back in Indiana sent money for a stone to be erected. In addition to Bass's name and dates of birth and death, it said "A brave man reposes in death here / Why was he not true?" That question suggests his family did know something of his life of crime.

Sam met his fate at Round Rock, July the twenty-first,
They pierced poor Sam with rifle balls and emptied out his
* purse.*
Poor Sam he is a corpse and six foot under clay,
And Jackson's in the bushes trying to get away.

Jackson did get away and made it back to Denton County. There he looked for Murphy, planning to murder him if he could find him. Even though Murphy was his cousin and Jackson had vouched for him, Jackson now considered Murphy to be an ingrate whose actions were unforgivable.

Figuring that Jackson would be out to avenge the deaths of Bass and Barnes, Murphy lived for almost a year in constant fear, frequently asking to spend his nights in the Denton County jail. When a doctor gave him some medicine to treat an eye infection in June of 1879, Murphy was cautioned to be careful with the liquid as it contained belladonna and was deadly poison if ingested. He took his own life by drinking the entire contents. He was dead in a matter of hours. Jackson simply disappeared—unless a rumor is true that he lived out his life on a ranch in New Mexico.

Perhaps it was remorse as much as fear that drove Murphy to suicide, for Bass had been as generous with him as he was with everyone else.

Jim had borrowed Sam's good gold and didn't want to pay,
The only shot he saw was to give poor Sam away.
He sold out Sam and Barnes and left their friends to mourn—
Oh, what a scorching Jim will get when Gabriel blows his
    horn!

Gillett says Murphy had hesitated, at first, when asked to betray his leader. Bass "had been kind to his family, had given them money and provisions." Murphy acknowledged that "it would be ungrateful to betray his friend." Only the warning that the overwhelming evidence against him was sure to send Murphy to federal prison—probably for life—finally convinced him to cooperate with the Rangers.

And so he sold out Sam and Barnes and left their
    friends to mourn.
Oh, what a scorching Jim will get when Gabriel blows his
    horn!
Perhaps he's got to heaven, there's none of us can say,
But if I'm right in my surmise he's gone the other way.

The repetition of the line about the "scorching Jim will get" leaves no doubt about where the balladeer's sympathies lie.

Although Jim Matthews says that Bass "was known as a man with no scruples who thought nothing of gunning down a man for a plug of tobacco," the general consensus among his biographers is that, save for Deputy Grimes, Bass and his gang never killed anyone. That does not mean Bass was not a good shot, according to Dobie, who passes on another bit of legendary lore about Bass's skill as a marksman: "While galloping by a live oak tree near Belton, they say, he [Bass] six-shootered his initials into it."

Aside from the ten thousand dollars he got from the Union Pacific train robbery, Bass never gathered in enough loot to be considered much of a success as an outlaw. On his way to Round Rock and his final showdown with the Rangers, he spent his last twenty-dollar gold piece, reportedly saying it was "the last of the 1877 gold" taken off the Union Pacific. "It hasn't done me a bit of good, but easy come, easy go—I'll get some more where that came from." He had, earlier in the spring, laid down two of the twenty-dollar gold pieces at a dry-goods store in Kaufman. He asked the clerk to fit him with a good suit. The clerk, a young man named Chunk Porter, was able to do that and went to the safe to get Bass his change. Porter worked the combination, opened the safe door, and pulled out a tray full of money. Bass, meanwhile, had put on the new suit and was standing at Porter's side. Porter had no idea who he was. "Son," said the man, "that is a good deal of money." He advised Porter not to let everybody who came by see how much money was in the safe. Then the man mounted up and rode away with his companions. After Bass was killed in Round Rock, the suit he wore was identified as having come from the dry-goods store in Kaufman, and yet he had bypassed the chance to rob the place.

So it seems unlikely that Bass left buried treasure behind, even though legends of that sort persist, especially in central Texas. He simply did not have any treasure to bury. What he did leave behind were stories and a chance for a balladeer to perpetuate a legend about the Texas Robin Hood.

CHAPTER NINE
John Wesley Hardin
Gunslinger Lawyer

John Wesley Hardin was a preacher's kid who claimed he never killed anyone who didn't need killing. Hardin's father was a sometimes circuit-riding Methodist who named his second surviving son of ten children after the founder of the Methodist faith, John Wesley. But it would be a good long while before the Texas John Wesley would "get religion."

Most of his biographers simply tick off the men Hardin allegedly killed, starting with an ex-slave named Mage. According to Hardin's own account of the shooting, it happened when he was fifteen, in November of 1868, after he challenged Mage to a wrestling match and won, badly scratching Mage's face. According to excerpts from Hardin's autobiography, published after his death, the next day a vengeful Mage came at him and struck him with a big stick. As he did, Hardin says, "I pulled out a Colt's .44 six-shooter and told him to get back." But Mage grabbed hold of Hardin's horse's bridle until Hardin shot Mage down. Hardin went to get his uncle and another man. When they returned, Mage was still alive and "still showed fight." Had it not been for his uncle, Hardin says, "I would have shot him [Mage] again." The uncle gave Hardin a twenty-dollar gold piece and sent him home to tell his father. Mage died shortly thereafter. "This was the first man I ever killed," Hardin says, "and it nearly distracted my father and mother when I told them."

Historian James M. Smallwood tells that story another way. He says one of Hardin's uncles, Barnett Hardin, arranged the wrestling match, just for "a little extra entertainment," between two teenagers—John Wesley and a young friend—and the ex-slave, Mage. In this version, "the mature, hard-muscled freedman"

John Wesley Hardin: Gunslinger Lawyer
WESTERN HISTORY COLLECTIONS AT THE UNIVERSITY OF OKLAHOMA

won two matches with the boys, and John Wesley took the defeats hard, especially because Mage was black and supposedly "inferior" to his white combatants. For Hardin grew up among people who believed in white supremacy and in the mental inferiority of blacks, and, apparently, "he never questioned such 'truths'; rather he internalized them."

Whatever his motive, Smallwood says, Hardin went hunting for Mage the day after the wrestling matches, armed with a Colt .44. When he found Mage on a pathway in a wooded area, Hardin "emptied all the rounds from the Colt into the freedman, leaving him mortally wounded but alive." That's when Hardin sought the counsel of his uncle Claiborne Holshousen, a local judge, spinning the tale about Mage's aggression in an attempt to justify the shooting. Young Hardin, his uncle, and one of the judge's neighbors went to the scene of the shooting and heard Mage's side of the story. The enraged Hardin wanted to shoot Mage again, but his uncle prevented that. The judge did turn over the twenty-dollar gold piece, and Hardin did tell his father. Mage died the next day.

Worried that the Yankee occupation forces in the Reconstruction South would deal harshly with his son for killing a black man, Hardin's father told him to go into hiding. This was Texas, after all, and "Texas, like other states, was then overrun with carpetbaggers and bureau agents who had the United States Army to back them up in their meanness." That was Hardin's opinion, once again showing that he was clearly a son of the old South where "the justice of the Southern cause" had been taught to him as a youth. He never relinquished those teachings, he says, and was true to his early training. "The way you bend a twig, that is the way it will grow, is an old saying, and a true one. So I grew up a rebel," he says.

In his eyes then, Hardin became a fugitive, "not from justice, but from the injustice and misrule of the people who subjugated the South." Both Hardin and his father believed that to be tried "at that time for the killing of a Negro meant certain death at the hands of a court, backed by Northern bayonets."

Truth be told, however, Hardin had shown signs of violence even before he committed his first murder. His father had taken up school teaching and was headmaster of a school John Wesley attended in 1867. The boy's quick temper and willingness to fight were demonstrated on at least two occasions at the school. Smallwood records one instance in which Hardin, wielding an open pocketknife, "threatened to kill one of his teachers because the instructor was preparing to spank one of his friends." In another, a youngster challenged Hardin, and Hardin almost killed the boy, "stabbing him in the back and chest." John Wesley "justified his act by claiming that the boy had used vulgarity in speaking about a girl." As C. L. Sonnichsen observes, Hardin "never saw anything bad in what he did."

After Mage's murder, Hardin fled to his brother's house at Logallis Prairie, a small community about twenty-five miles north of Sumpter, Texas, where in December of 1868 he claimed to have killed three Union soldiers who sought to arrest him. In his account, Hardin set up an ambush at the Hickory Creek crossing, having decided to take the fight to his perceived enemies: "I waylaid them," he says, "as I had no mercy on men whom I knew only wanted to get my body to torture and kill. It was war to the knife for me, and I brought it on by opening the fight with a double-barreled shotgun and ended it with a cap and ball six-shooter. Thus it was by the fall of 1868 I had killed four men and was myself wounded in the arm." He says he knocked two of the men off their horses with shotgun blasts and then shot the third with the Colt after that man had wounded Hardin on his left arm.

Again, Smallwood questions Hardin's version, saying that there is no documented evidence that three federal troopers died in the area during December 1868. Therefore, Smallwood says, Hardin's tale may be "fanciful." Oh, it may well be true that Hardin killed three men who were on his trail, but they were most likely Texas lawmen, and Hardin simply substituted the hated Yankees as his victims "because they deserved it," in his mind.

On the run again, he went to the home of a widowed aunt in Navarro County, south of Corsicana. His aunt opened a one-room log cabin school at Pisgah Ridge, where Hardin taught the basic "3 Rs" to a class of twenty-five. He also practiced his shooting skills in his spare time, especially with handguns, and he began to gamble and to drink to excess. He gained a reputation for being "a mean drunk who often went looking for trouble." After the three-month school term, he moved on to another uncle's place in Richland Bottom in the same area. His older cousins there were cattle drovers and taught him the cowboy's trade.

Within a year, according to Hardin's scorekeeping, he had killed another soldier there at Richland Bottom while he was riding with one of his cousins, Simpson "Simp" Dixon, a Ku Klux Klan member and another hater of Yankees. The two engaged in a gunfight with Yankee soldiers and killed two of them, presumably one each.

On Christmas in 1869 Hardin was in a card game with a man named Jim Bradley in Towash, Hill County, Texas. To hear him tell it, Hardin was winning almost every hand, and Bradley was getting angrier and angrier. The two later squared off in a gunfight egged on by a crowd. In Hardin's account,

> Bradley saw me and tried to cut me off, getting in front of me with a pistol in one hand and a Bowie knife in the other. He commenced to fire on me, firing once, then snapping, and then firing again. By this time we were within five or six feet of each other, and I fired a Remington .45 at his heart and right after that at his head. As he staggered and fell, he said, "O, Lordy, don't shoot me any more."

Hardin admits he did not stop shooting, however, because he was concerned about what the crowd might do; he "did not want to take chances on a reaction." But, he says, the crowd ran, and he "stood there and cursed them loud and long as cowardly devils who had urged a man to fight and when he did and fell, to desert him like cowards and traitors."

This time within a month he had claimed another victim, and once again, there is some debate about what motivated the shooting. This one happened in Limestone County at Horn Hill, where a circus was encamped. In his autobiography, Hardin says a circus employee struck him and that the retaliation was therefore justified. According to a witness, however, Hardin had slipped under the circus tent in an attempt to enter without paying. A security guard saw him, caught him, and intended to throw him out. Hardin's response was to pull his revolver and murder the guard. The details will remain sketchy at best, suggests Smallwood, "for Hardin always justified all his killings by blaming the victims."

The story Hardin records in his autobiography about a killing in Kosse, a railroad town in southwestern Limestone County, has him outsmarting a man who tried to rob him:

> I told him that I only had about $50 or $60 in my pocket but if he would go with me to the stable I would give him more, as I had money in my saddle pocket. . . . He said, "Give me what you have first." I told him all right, and in so doing, dropped some of it on the floor. He stooped down to pick it up and as he was straightening up I pulled my pistol and fired. The ball struck him between the eyes and he fell over, a dead robber.

Another version leaves not a dead robber but a dead pimp, one of whose prostitutes had caught Hardin's fancy. In that version, Hardin had met and spent several nights in the company of the local girl at the Three Star Saloon in Kosse. Her "manager" was a man named Comstock who may have been jealous or who may have been demanding money owed for the girl's services. In any event, harsh words passed between the two men, and Hardin shot Comstock in the head.

By this time, not only the military but also the Texas Rangers were on Hardin's trail, so he headed northeasterly and crossed over into Louisiana. He began using an alias and invented a new past for himself. In the fall of 1870, however, he returned to central Texas and stirred up more trouble in Waco. As was his pattern now, he fell in with a rough crowd and began running with a band of about a dozen lawless men. Before the turn of the new year, Hardin had killed another man, L. J. Hoffman, a US deputy marshal who recognized Hardin in a barbershop. A shoot-out followed, leaving Hoffman dead on the floor.

Hardin fled northeast again and got as far as the East Texas town of Longview. This time the law caught up with him, and he was arrested by a state policeman on January 9, 1871, and charged with four counts of murder and one count of horse theft. He was to stand trial for Hoffman's murder back in Waco. While he was in jail in Longview, Hardin bought a smuggled-in Colt .45 from one of his cell mates and used it to kill a state policeman guard and escape during the trip to Waco. Taking the policeman's horse, Hardin rode for his parents' house in the Hill County town of Mount Calm. The circumstances were not the least "calm," of course, and once again Hardin's father urged his son to run for it, this time to Mexico. John Wesley didn't even make it as far as Belton before he was arrested again. Three state officers planned to take Hardin to Austin but camped for the night about ten miles south of Belton. They rotated guard duty, but one of the guards fell asleep and Hardin stayed awake. He grabbed a double-barreled shotgun and killed two of the men; then he killed the third with a pistol.

He went back to his parents' house again, telling "his father of his newest troubles and newest murders while, of course, spinning the story to make himself appear blameless," as Smallwood says. His father may or may not have believed Hardin but gave the same advice as before: Go south, and do not stop until you reach Mexico. John Wesley headed south all right, but then he veered off to the southeast toward Gonzales. He had relatives there, and relatives' homes always seemed to be his places of refuge. This time it was the Clements clan, cousins on his father's side. Once again Hardin was introduced to the cowboy life as his cousins were contractors who drove cattle herds up the Chisholm Trail to the railhead at Abilene, Kansas.

The Clements kin suggested he hire on as a trail boss, giving him an opportunity to get out of Texas long enough for things to cool down, so in 1871 Hardin went as a cowboy up the Chisholm Trail. He is said to have killed as many as seven people en route (Hardin claims only five in his autobiography) and three in Abilene, Kansas. Smallwood says Hardin "may well have been the most dangerous man to ever go up the Chisholm Trail." He killed so many men "he proved to be psychotic, a pathological sociopath, a professional killing machine," but, as always, "he blamed others for his deeds while he killed methodically and remorselessly."

Not all the chroniclers of Hardin's life are quite so hard on the gunfighter. C. F. Eckhardt, who says he gathered information from the nephew of a man who rode with Hardin, says Hardin never killed anyone except in a "fair fight." Joe Tom Davis too seems to defend Hardin against his detractors, saying, "He was not a typical gunfighter: He killed only in self-defense. . . ." Davis characterizes Hardin as "a gentleman in appearance and manners, intelligent and polite, and a doting but absentee father who tried to instill high ideals in his children." According to Eckhardt, his informant, Ernst Duderstadt, said his uncle, Fred Duderstadt, was Hardin's closest friend and rode with him as a cowboy. Hardin was Wes to Fred, as he was to almost everyone except his mother, who called him Johnny. Eckhardt says that once Hardin hired on as a cowboy, "his regular line of business was trailing cattle north."

However, that didn't keep him out of mischief, apparently. Hardin recounts one episode on the trail in February 1871 when some of the cowboys took him to "a Mexican camp where they were dealing monte." Saying he "soon learned the rudiments of the game," Hardin began to bet with the rest. When the dealer refused to pay him for a winner, Hardin says, "I struck him over the head with my pistol as he was drawing a knife, shot another as he also was drawing a knife." As if to affirm and justify his actions, Hardin remarks, "The best people in the vicinity said I did a good thing."

Once in Abilene, Hardin encountered city marshal "Wild Bill" Hickok, who dubbed Hardin "Little Arkansas," judging him to be both young and "green." Of course, in his account of their meeting, Hardin is the one who backs down Hickok. Describing Abilene as a "fast town," Hardin says he spent most of his time there "in the saloons and gambling houses." One day while Hardin was drinking and rolling ten pins with several Texans in a saloon, Hickok came in to say they were making too much noise. Hickok also told Hardin to remove his pistols until he was ready to leave town. Rather than relinquish the pistols, Hardin followed Hickok out into the street. Finally, according to Hardin, Hickok pulled his pistol and said, "Take those pistols off. I arrest you." Hardin says he pulled his pistols from their scabbards but "reversed them and whirled them over on him [Hickok] with the muzzles in his face. . . . I told him to put his pistols up, which he did." Hardin quotes Hickok as saying, "You are the gamest and quickest boy I ever saw. Let us compromise this matter and I will be your friend."

One of the most often listed of Hardin's alleged killings comes from the time he spent in Abilene. Paul Trachtman calls it "one of Hardin's most callous crimes, so ignoble that even he showed some faint sign of shame and attempted to pass it off as a justifiable shooting of a man who was trying to steal his pants." The story is that Hardin was staying at the American House Hotel in Abilene and "began firing bullets through a bedroom wall simply to stop the snoring of a stranger in the next room." The first bullet woke the man; the second killed him. Trachtman quotes Hardin as saying, years later, "They say I killed six or seven men for snoring. Well, it ain't true. I only killed one man for snoring." Eckhardt says Hardin "never shot anyone 'for snoring too loud,'" and he cites Fred Duderstadt's recollections as evidence. Duderstadt remembered that, on the night in question, he and Hardin "were with a herd about fifty miles north" of Abilene. So it remains Hardin's own word against that of his friend Duderstadt.

Although Hardin never settled down, he did get married to Jane Bowen in March 1872, and they lived for a time on Fred

Duderstadt's ranch back in Gonzales County in Texas. Hardin can't have been much of a family man, since he was running from lawmen most of the time, but the couple did have three children: a son and two daughters.

Meanwhile, Hardin got into difficulty with Governor Edmund J. Davis's State Police. Davis was determined to shut down the gang building a criminal empire in south-central Texas. That would be the Taylor ring, or Taylor's raiders, anti-Reconstructionist forces led by John Taylor, a relative of Hardin's. In time the Taylor gang became the Hardin-Taylor gang, and the murder rate attributed to the ring went up considerably. For one thing, the Taylors were feuding with the Suttons. They represented two of the largest cattle families in DeWitt County, and they first "fell into disagreement over cattle on certain portions of the range," as C. L. Douglas puts it. The disagreements escalated into killings on both sides, including Hardin's shooting of Jack Helms, a US marshal thought to be sympathetic to the Suttons. Hardin also shot Special Policeman Green Paramore, a black officer ordered to look for Hardin in Gonzales County, and wounded another black officer named Lackey. Governor Davis offered a four-thousand-dollar reward for "Wesley Clements" (one of Hardin's aliases). According to Smallwood, however, "Despite the lure of a reward to bounty hunters, Hardin never served a day in jail or in prison for the murder of Paramore and the attempted murder of Lackey."

Hardin was finally captured in July 1877 in Florida, tried for a murder he committed in 1874, and sentenced in 1878 to twenty-five years in prison. It was on his twenty-first birthday, May 26, 1874, that Hardin had shot and killed Brown County Deputy Sheriff Charles Webb. Hardin and some friends were celebrating in Comanche, Texas, when Webb approached. Reports are that Hardin asked if Webb had come to arrest him. Webb said no, and Hardin invited him into the hotel for a drink. Following Hardin inside, Webb drew his gun; one of Hardin's men yelled a warning; Hardin spun around, drew his own guns, and Webb was shot dead. Hardin got away, but a lynch mob hanged his brother Joe and two cousins.

While in Huntsville Prison, Hardin was at first stubborn, sullen, and vicious. He made several attempts to escape, but after about five years he seemed to adapt to prison life and used his time to better himself. He read theological books and was superintendent of the prison Sunday school. He studied law. By the time he was released from prison in February 1894, after serving almost sixteen years of his sentence, he was a forty-one-year-old widower, his wife having died in 1892. Within six months of his release, he was pardoned.

He went back to Gonzales. In July 1894 he passed the state's bar examination and was licensed to practice law. In 1895 he went to El Paso to testify for the defense in a murder trial and stayed, establishing a law practice there. Just when he seemed to be going straight, however, he apparently took up with one of his married female clients. Her husband didn't take kindly to the affair, and Hardin may have tried hiring some law officials to kill him. If that is the case, one of the hired gunmen, Constable John Selman, killed Hardin instead. Hardin was shooting dice in the Acme Saloon on August 19, 1895, when Selman came up behind him and shot him in the head. Another version of the deadly dispute is that Selman's son, John Selman Jr., also an El Paso lawman, had arrested Hardin's lady friend, prompting an argument between the younger Selman and Hardin. The older Selman approached Hardin on the afternoon of the shooting, and the two of them exchanged words. Shortly before midnight Selman Sr. entered the Acme Bar and shot Hardin. Whatever the motive, Hardin met his end in the same violent circumstances he'd been a part of much of his life.

Prompted by what must be a peculiar fascination with notorious outlaws, these days, Davis says, "a steady stream of visitors come to the abandoned part of old Concordia Cemetery [in El Paso] to pay homage at the grave of a legend," John Wesley Hardin.

CHAPTER TEN

O. Henry
Writer of Stories

William Sidney Porter came to Texas for his health. He left sixteen years later a convicted embezzler bound for a federal prison in Ohio. He never came back to Texas but drew heavily on his experiences there as the successful writer O. Henry.

Born on the outskirts of Greensboro, North Carolina, September 11, 1862, Porter was the son of a respected physician and an artistic mother. His mother died when he was barely three, and he was reared by his paternal grandmother and schooled by an aunt who inspired his great love of reading and storytelling.

During his youth he was plagued by a persistent cough that concerned a family friend, Dr. James Hall. The fear was that young Will's cough might signal the onset of tuberculosis—or consumption, as it was called in those days—the disease that had killed his mother. Dr. Hall's four sons worked on a large ranch near Cotulla, Texas, and the Halls prevailed on Porter, now nineteen, to come with them for a visit, believing that the dry air would help Porter's lungs. Dr. Hall's oldest son, Lee, managed the guest ranch in La Salle County, and the younger brothers all worked there. One of them, Richard, invited Porter to stay with him and his family, and Will's visit stretched to two years. He hired on as a ranch hand and learned to rope and brand cattle and to herd sheep. His health improved, and he thrived as he participated in outdoor activities at the ranch.

One of his jobs was to ride his dun pony once a week fourteen miles one way to pick up the mail at Fort Ewell. It was a daylong round-trip: four hours there, four hours back. As one who apparently loved to roam, he took in everything about the landscape and the people, learning the names of plants and trees such as live oak,

O. Henry: Writer of Stories
AUSTIN HISTORY CENTER

chaparral, mesquite, Spanish dagger, hackberry, and prickly pear. He also began learning to speak Spanish and to play the guitar.

When the Halls moved to another ranch in 1884, Porter traveled with them as far as Austin, the state capital, and there he remained, staying first with the Joseph Harrell family, also friends from North Carolina. He continued to draw, play his guitar, and sing, spending more time in these artistic pursuits than he did in working. He sang bass with the Hill City Quartette, in three church choirs, and in various theater productions in Austin. In time he did take a steady job as a bookkeeper and then became an assistant draftsman in the General Land Office, the latter appointment gained with help from his old friend Richard Hall, recently named Texas land commissioner.

In 1887 Porter married Athol Estes Roach, a seventeen-year-old he had first seen placing mementos on behalf of her classmates in the cornerstone of the new state capitol. Athol's mother did not approve of the match, but Porter persuaded Athol to elope with him shortly after she graduated. He was twenty-four.

Athol shared his love of music—they both sang in the Southern Presbyterian Church choir—and encouraged Porter to write and submit stories and sketches. He sold his first story for six dollars, but he didn't quit his day job, which, at that time, was still in the General Land Office. He and Athol had two children, a son, Anson, who died soon after birth, and a daughter, Margaret. In 1891 he lost his appointed job when a new administration brought about changes at the Land Office, and now, with a wife and daughter to support, he needed another one soon.

A friend, Charles Anderson, helped Porter get hired as a teller at the First National Bank in Austin. Whereas Will had enjoyed his surroundings, his colleagues, and the fast pace of work during his four years at the Land Office, he did not take to banking, even though it paid him the same hundred-dollar-a-month salary he'd been getting. His new tasks—taking deposits, cashing checks and drafts, and keeping books on his transactions—he found boring. He would amuse himself during slow periods by drawing sketches, something he had also done in the margins of the maps he worked on in the Land Office.

He put his drawing and writing skills to more public use when he started his own weekly comic magazine, *The Rolling Stone,* in 1894. It lasted only a year, but it set him on a path to being a writer. Meanwhile, he resigned from his job at the bank in December of 1894, became a columnist at the Houston *Post* in 1895, and was subsequently charged with embezzlement of bank funds dating back to the time he was a teller at First National Bank. He was arrested early in 1896 but released on bond pending a trial date set for July. Settling his wife and daughter with Athol's parents in Austin, Porter continued to write for the Houston *Post* until he skipped town just before his trial was to begin and fled first to New Orleans and then to Honduras, a country with no extradition treaty with the United States.

In less than a year, however, Porter returned to Austin voluntarily when he received word that Athol was dying of tuberculosis. He turned himself in to face trial but devoted himself to helping care for his wife until she died on July 25, 1897, at age twenty-nine. His trial began in February of 1898, and he made little effort to defend himself other than to maintain throughout that he was innocent. The jury found him guilty of embezzling $854.08, and he was sentenced to five years, to be served at the Ohio State Penitentiary. Already altering his name to obscure his identity, he changed the spelling of his middle name from "Sidney" to "Sydney" and began using it rather than "William" or "Will." His in-laws promised to take care of Margaret and to keep her from knowing that her father was in prison. They moved from Texas to Pittsburgh, Pennsylvania.

Just how guilty of the embezzlement charges Porter may have been is still being debated. In a biographical blurb about him in *A Treasury of American Literature,* the editors state, unequivocally, "Certainly innocent, as subsequent investigation has proved, and on his way to stand trial, he took the wrong train at a junction, fled to Central America, and spent a fantastic year at sea and on land with smugglers and outlaws." There would seem to be more than a little creative license in that assessment. No investigative proof has totally absolved Porter, and it is doubtful that taking "the wrong train at a junction" would cause him to wind up in Honduras. According to biographer Peggy Caravantes, "The jury had deliberated for only an hour when it returned with a guilty verdict." For one thing, jurors "had a hard time believing that an innocent man would have run away." About all Porter had to say in the aftermath was what he wrote in a letter to his mother-in-law: "I am absolutely innocent of wrong-doing in the bank matter, except so far as foolishly keeping a position that I could not successfully fill."

Later researchers have pointed out that banking practices in the late nineteenth century were fairly slipshod and that Porter may have been nothing more than a victim of his own or others' carelessness. Two brothers named Brackenridge managed the bank "very casually," says Caravantes, allowing customers "to write checks even when there was no money in their accounts." Furthermore, bank employees themselves "helped themselves to money whenever they needed it, sometimes putting an IOU in the cash drawer, sometimes not." She relates one instance in which Porter "spent days searching for missing money until a bank official walked by and said: 'Porter, I took out $300 last week. See if I left a memo; I meant to.'"

O. Henry scholar Trueman E. O'Quinn, himself an attorney and judge, examined court records and read banking reports and other documents pertaining to Porter's case. He points out that a bookkeeper who preceded Porter at the bank "had embezzled or 'borrowed' some funds he could not repay." Perhaps because he was a relative, the Brackenridge brothers dismissed him from his post but did not prosecute. They made up the loss by "levying an assessment on the stockholders" and asked a bank examiner to keep quiet about the discrepancies and the cover-up.

When federal bank examiner F. B. Gray discovered shortages in accounts managed by Porter in 1894, however, he believed he had "compelling evidence" that Porter had embezzled money on a number of occasions. Once again, the bank's owners took responsibility and did not want to prosecute. They admitted to their "loose banking practices" and even brought in J. M. Thornton, the relative who had preceded Porter, to testify that there had been discrepancies before Porter took over the job. The grand jury, therefore, decided there was not enough evidence to charge Porter and no-billed him. That could have been the end of the matter but for the fact that Gray did not keep quiet; in fact, he persisted and sought a federal indictment. The investigation was reopened under direct orders from the comptroller of currency in Washington DC, and Porter faced five charges of embezzling a total of $5,487.02 over the course of several months. His father-in-law and a friend posted bond and offered to make up the five-thousand-dollar deficit. Gray would have none of it and insisted that Porter stand trial.

As Caravantes points out, "no one knows for certain if Porter simply mismanaged his bookkeeping or whether he withdrew small sums with the intention of paying them back or just stole them." One of Porter's friends would say later that Porter told her he knew who was taking the money, although he wouldn't give a name. This person was a good friend, Porter said, someone he trusted "would straighten matters out if given time." If that is true, the friend did not straighten matters out, and it would appear that Porter was willing to take the rap for him or her. Porter made no attempt to implicate anyone else during his trial.

By the time Porter's trial began, the prosecution had dropped all but two charges, bringing the embezzlement total down to $854.08. Even though, as Trueman notes, "the prosecution could never prove that Will Porter actually had possession of any monies taken from bank funds—only that there were undisputed mixups and flaws in bookkeeping for which he was responsible," he was convicted. His fleeing the country "made it difficult for the jury to acquit." Porter himself recognized that his flight suggested an admission of guilt and was a fatal error: "I am like Lord Jim," he said, "because we both made one fateful mistake at the supreme crisis of our lives, a mistake from which we could not recover."

Later, as O. Henry, Porter would make use of his experiences and caricature the bank examiner out to "get his man" in "Friends in San Rosario." In the story Gray becomes J. F. C. Nettlewick, whose "air denoted a quiet but conscious reserve force, if not actual authority." Nettlewick questions the fictional bank teller, Perry Dorsey, "concerning each of the cash memoranda . . . with unimpeachable courtesy, yet with something so mysteriously momentous in his frigid manner that the teller was reduced to pink cheeks and a stammering tongue." Thinking he has found discrepancies in the bank's documentation of loan securities, the examiner goes after the bank president, feeling "a slight thrill" in doing so. Nettlewick thinks to himself:

> There would be no leaving San Rosario for him that day. He would have to telegraph to the Comptroller of the Currency; he would have to swear out a warrant before the United States Commissioner for the arrest of Major Kingman [the bank president]; perhaps he would be ordered to close the bank on account of the loss of the securities. It was not the first crime the examiner had unearthed. Once or twice the terrible upheaval of human emotions that his investigations had loosed had almost caused a ripple in his official calm. He had seen bank men kneel and plead and cry like women for a chance—an hour's time—the overlooking of a single error.

Porter's story has a happier ending than his real-life episode, and the banker outsmarts the examiner.

Two other stories, "A Call Loan" and "The Guardian of the Scutcheon" (the latter retitled "The Guardian of the Accolade"), allude to the casual banking practices of the time. In "A Call Loan" there once again appears a "thorough" bank examiner, this one described as "a dyspeptic man, wearing double-magnifying glasses." In none of these stories, however, is there a tone of bitterness or accusation. They are as balanced and full of good humor as any of O. Henry's other works.

Porter's own "fateful mistake" of running way before his first trial date may have been the impetus for a story about an escaping embezzler who has second thoughts in New Orleans. In "Blind Man's Holiday," the protagonist, Lorison (formerly Larsen), sees himself as "an outcast from society, forever to be a shady skulker along the ragged edge of respectability." He confesses to his lady love that he is "wrongly accused of one crime" but, he believes, "guilty of another." This story, too, has a happy, if typically unpredictable, ending as Lorison wins the lady's hand and there is every promise that he and she will live happily ever after.

Porter served only three years and three months of his five-year sentence in Ohio and did not spend his time sitting in a prison cell. Instead, he worked first as the night pharmacist in the prison hospital, returning to a profession he had practiced as a young man in his uncle's drugstore back in North Carolina. He spent the remainder of his time, perhaps ironically, as the bookkeeper for the prison steward. Peter Glassman observes that rather than breaking his spirit, "prison seemed to inspire Porter. Drawing on the many people he had met in his travels and the colorful characters he now met behind bars, he began to write and submit stories to small magazines under the pen name O. Henry."

Of the several versions of how Porter came by his pseudonym, one has its roots in Austin during the time he was rooming with the Joseph Harrell family in Texas. It says he derived the name from his frequent calling of "Oh, Henry," the family cat. According to Paul Horowitz, one report says that "as early as 1885, [Porter] used the name to sign a poem, 'A Soliloquy by the Cat,'" and that Porter himself had a cat named Henry the Proud. Most other accounts suggest that he settled on the name when he most needed it: after his conviction when he was trying to keep his past identity a secret. The two most often cited say that he acquired the name either from a prison warden called Orrin Henry or from the abbreviation of the name of an eminent French pharmacist, Etienne Ossian Henry, found in the *U. S. Dispensatory,* a reference work Porter used when he was in the prison pharmacy. Porter once said he found the name in the society column of a New Orleans newspaper.

Released from prison for good behavior in 1901, Porter had no reason to return to Texas. He went instead to Pittsburgh, Pennsylvania, where his in-laws had moved with his daughter, Margaret. He had no desire to stay in Pittsburgh either, although he lived there for almost a year and worked for a newspaper while he was still turning out short stories at a furious pace. He described Pittsburgh as "the low-downdest hole on the surface of the earth." In 1902 he moved to New York City, where he reached the height of his career and became the most widely read short story writer of his time. In 1907 he married Sara Lindsay Coleman, a childhood friend from Greensboro, North Carolina. They separated within a year, in part because of Porter's heavy drinking and deteriorating health. He died in New York on June 5, 1910, of diabetes mellitus complicated by cirrhosis of the liver. His last recorded words were, "Turn up the lights. I don't want to go home in the dark," lines remembered from a song.

Although Porter never physically returned to Texas after he was released from prison, he certainly went back to the storehouse of material he had gathered there as he created more than fifty stories—some estimates are up to eighty—with a Texas setting. A number of them were collected in *The Heart of the West* (1907). They drew on his experiences at the sheep ranch, the land office, the bank in Austin, and the Houston *Post.* The knowledge of ranch life that Porter gained was incorporated into the stories, as was his familiarity with Mexican dialect. He developed more than two hundred fifty characters, at least some of them, no doubt, based on Texans he had known. For example, Lee Hall, a former Texas Ranger and manager of the south Texas ranch Porter first came to, became the prototype for the Texas Ranger who appears in many of the tales. In "The Caballero's Way," he introduced the Cisco Kid, a fictitious desperado later appropriated by Hollywood movie and television productions and transformed into a more heroic Mexican caballero.

Even more striking than his characters are the settings Porter developed. The sensory details remembered from his time on the Texas coastal plains, in particular, create vivid pictures, as in this passage from "Hygeia at the Solito":

> *They sped upon velvety wheels across an exhilarant savanna. The pair of Spanish ponies struck a nimble, tireless trot, which gait they occasionally relieved by a wild, untrammeled gallop. The air was wine and seltzer, perfumed, as they absorbed it, with the delicate redolence of prairie flowers. The road perished, and the buckboard swam the uncharted billows of the grass itself.*

The sheer size of the state is the focus at the beginning of "A Departmental Case." Porter says, "In Texas you may travel a thousand miles in a straight line." Of one county, he adds, "I have forgotten how many New Jerseys and Rhode Islands it was that could have been stowed away and lost in its chaparral." And all of this is merely "to hint that the big ex-republic of the Southwest forms a sizable star on the flag, and to prepare for the corollary that things sometimes happen there uncut to pattern and unfettered by metes and bounds."

In all, Porter published hundreds of stories and gained fame as one of America's favorite short story writers before his death at age forty-seven. Horowitz synthesizes what a number of biographers and literary critics have determined about the sources for his writing:

> *O. Henry used his life experiences as the basis for his stories, and the knowledgeable reader can, indeed, find autobiographical references in much of his writing. He sometimes buries or disguises these references, but at other times they*

stand out clearly. Fiction, he felt, was the best vehicle for "getting at" reality. In a letter to an editor who had written an article in praise of his work, O. Henry stated that "most autobiographies are insincere from beginning to end. About the only chance for truth to be told is in fiction."

As it turned out, the stranger-than-fiction truth of his own life had something of a twist at the end he so favored in his own stories. For by losing his freedom, in one sense, he gained it in another as his incarceration on the embezzlement charge finally gave him the time to write. And his move from Texas to the northeast was not entire as he took with him the memories that provided material for his first stories. He likely appreciated the irony.

CHAPTER ELEVEN

Gregorio Cortez
Man on the Run

In the summer of 1901 two brothers, Gregorio and Romaldo Cortez, were farming on land they had rented from W. A. Thulemeyer. Thulemeyer's ranch was about ten miles west of Kenedy in south-central Texas. The brothers' corn crop was tall and looked promising for a good harvest. Having finished their noon meal on June 12, a hot, clear day, they rested on Gregorio's front porch in the company of their mother and their wives. Gregorio's four children were still inside eating. Sheriff W. T. "Brack" Morris, of Karnes County, and one of his deputies, Boone Choate, rode in a surrey up to the gate in front of the house. Another deputy, John Trimmell, had stationed himself near some pens and a gate with several roads leading away from it.

Romaldo went out to greet the two men in the surrey, then turned and called to Gregorio, *Te quieren,* literally, "you are wanted," or, in general terms, "Someone wants to talk to you." Deputy Choate, spoke enough Spanish to act as interpreter, but he didn't always get things quite straight. According to Américo Paredes, Choate thought Romaldo's "you are wanted" statement indicated "that both Cortezes knew that Gregorio was a wanted man." For the sheriff and his deputies were on the trail of a horse thief. They had been asked by the sheriff of Atascosa County to help find the culprit, but the only information Sheriff Morris had was that the suspect "was a medium-sized Mexican with a big broad-brimmed Mexican hat." Although no broad-brimmed hat was in evidence, Gregorio could be considered medium-size—small, really, and wiry. In addition, a Kenedy man, Andrés Villarreal, had told the lawmen that he had recently acquired a mare in a trade with Gregorio. They were checking out a possible lead.

Gregorio Cortez: Man on the Run
COURTESY OF TEXAS STATE LIBRARY & ARCHIVES COMMISSION

Gregorio joined Romaldo, both of them near the fence. Choate asked Gregorio if he had traded a horse, using the word *caballo,* to Villarreal. "No," Gregorio replied, since he had traded not a stallion, or male horse, but a *yegua,* a mare. He was not being contentious, only literal. That is when Sheriff Morris got out of the buggy and approached the Cortezes on the other side of the fence. Although he had no warrant, Morris told Choate to tell the brothers he was going to arrest them both. Choate translated the sheriff's statement. Gregorio answered in Spanish. What Choate heard was, "No white man can arrest me." What Gregorio more likely said was, "You can't arrest me for nothing."

The sheriff drew his pistol, and Romaldo, says Paredes, "ran at him, trying to protect his brother whom he thought unarmed like himself." Morris shot Romaldo. When Morris turned toward Gregorio, he saw that Gregorio did have a pistol, one he had slipped behind him when the surrey drew up. Morris fired in haste and missed. Gregorio shot immediately and did not miss. Still Morris was on his feet, firing wildly two or three more times before Gregorio shot him again. Morris began "to reel and stagger, going down the wire fence toward the gate." He fell, and Gregorio shot him once more as he lay on the ground. Choate ran into the chaparral "where it was the thickest" until he joined the other deputy a half mile away. Then they both retreated to Kenedy.

Gregorio ran too, but not very far—yet. He loaded his family, except for Romaldo, into a wagon and sent them to the house of a friend on the outskirts of town. He and his wounded brother then set out through the brush on horseback. The plan was to hide in the brush about halfway to town until dark and then slip into Kenedy to get medical help for Romaldo. Although a posse of fifty men or more combed the area, they never found the brothers, lying in the brush only five miles from Gregorio's house. Nor did they find Morris until the next morning as, wounded but still alive when the Cortezes left, he had made it to his feet and stumbled into the chaparral himself before he bled to death.

As soon as it got dark, the Cortez brothers resumed their flight to Kenedy, but it was slow going. Romaldo could no longer stay on his horse. Even when Gregorio abandoned his own horse and rode behind Romaldo on his to steady him, Romaldo kept slipping off. So Gregorio gave up on riding and carried his brother on foot, taking from dark until one o'clock in the morning to cover the remaining five miles to Kenedy. Once he deposited Romaldo with the family, Gregorio began his own flight, a trek that would be celebrated as legendary.

He started walking north, not south. He reckoned that his pursuers would expect him to ride for the border, and he was right. The posses all struck out for the Rio Grande. Cortez walked toward Gonzales County, about sixty-five miles away in a straight line. But Cortez did not walk in a straight line, so, according to Paredes, he "must have covered half again that distance," at least eighty miles, and he made it in about forty hours. That means he traveled "an average of two miles an hour for forty straight hours, through brush and other rough country; and for this hiking feat Cortez was wearing a pair of low-cut shoes with narrow, pointed toes." He was headed to Ottine and the Schnabel ranch, where he hoped to hide out with a friend named Martín Robledo. Cortez made it to the Robledos about sundown on June 14, and "one of the first things he did was to slip off his shoes." Robledo agreed to harbor Cortez for a few days, and, since the place "was in an isolated and wooded spot," Cortez was fairly confident that "he had fooled his pursuers."

But he hadn't accounted for Robert M. Glover, the sheriff of Gonzales County and a good friend of the late Sheriff Morris. Glover did not ride out pell-mell toward the Mexican border. Instead, he started asking questions, first in Karnes City, where Cortez's mother, wife, sister-in-law, and wounded brother had been put in jail. Even Cortez's children were there. One of the women— Glover did not say which one—was finally pressured into telling him where Cortez was going. Glover gathered up a posse on the way back to Gonzales. Among his recruits was Henry Schnabel, owner of the ranch on which the Robledos lived. The possemen were already hiding in the brush behind Robledo's house by the time Cortez was taking off his shoes on the front porch.

In Ottine, on their way to the ranch, the eight men in the posse bought a "black bottle" containing whiskey with which to fortify themselves, perhaps. Glover divided his posse in order to surround the south-facing house. He and another man approached the east side as one more came from the rear and five more took the west side. Their plan was to rush the house "in a run." The firing started on the southeast corner and was mostly between Glover, the only one still mounted, and Cortez. The others on the porch ran for the brush. Glover and Cortez kept exchanging fire until Glover fell dead from his horse; then Cortez ran for the brush as well and landed right in the middle of a patch of grass burrs. He was still barefoot. Tearing his vest in two, he bound the pieces on his feet and ran into a nearby field.

Heavy firing continued at the house, although the only ones left there were Mrs. Robledo and three young boys, all unarmed and inside. One of the possemen mistook one of the boys for a desperado and shot him; another fired blindly into the house and hit Mrs. Robledo. About the same time, Schnabel, one of the five men on the west side, was shot from close range, probably by one of his own inebriated comrades, and fell dead near the barn. When the shooting stopped, two possemen lay dead, and a woman and boy were wounded. A second boy, thirteen years old, was "hung up to a tree until his tongue protruded and his life was nearly extinct" as the posse tried to learn from him what the escapee's plans were. He did not tell because he did not know.

So now Cortez was hunted as the killer of two sheriffs, and he was on the run again. He did sneak back to Robledo's house after the shooting stopped and the law officers left and managed to get his shoes. He began walking, south this time, toward the Guadalupe River and the house of another friend, only ten miles away. By this time Cortez had walked nearly one hundred miles total. The friend, Ceferino Flores, gave Cortez a pistol, a sorrel mare, and a saddle. The posse showed up after Cortez rode away and gave Flores "the rope treatment"; he would later be sentenced to two years in prison for helping his friend escape.

The posse, with bloodhounds on the scent, chased Cortez across the Guadalupe River before they lost his trail. He continued to the San Antonio River, a distance of less than fifty miles in a straight line. Once again, however, he did not go in a straight line. Over a period of two days and one night he was "riding and riding, doubling back, stopping to shoot, then riding again, circling about, leaving false leads when he could, and riding again." In the beginning, the sorrel mare was "fleet and strong," but she began to show signs that she was giving out. A fresh posse picked up Cortez's trail, and the chase was on. For six hours he galloped his tired mount, "running in circles and zigzags in the area between Stockdale and Floresville." Sometimes the posse was only five hundred yards behind. Finally, the little mare could go no farther. She stopped and refused to take another step. Cortez barely had time to dismount before she fell dead.

After slipping the saddle and bridle off the mare, Cortez took cover "behind a thick tree trunk" and waited for the posse, which "stopped some distance away, dismounted, and broke into small groups." Somehow, even though he was still carrying the saddle and bridle, Cortez eluded his pursuers until dark by moving through the brush. He made his way to a pasture where he saw another mare, a small brown one. He caught her, saddled her, cut through the pasture fence with a file, mounted up, and rode for Cotulla. Later estimates were that he covered "at least three hundred miles in getting from Floresville to Cotulla, through brush and rough country, over barbed wire fences and rivers, in three days." J. Frank Dobie says:

> It was not speed that swirled in the consciousness of Gregorio Cortez as he fled on a little brown mare. What he remembered best long after the ride was the mare herself— her fidelity, her staying power, her generosity.

Throughout the chase, the mare made a name for herself. Paredes says, "Time and again posses sighted Cortez, and every time the mare ran away from them." The posses stopped for fresh horses and ran six to death.

By now, hundreds of men were out looking for Cortez. They had dogs, and they had the railroad. Certain that Cortez was headed for Laredo, lawmen transported fresh horses and more men up and down the tracks aboard trains running from Corpus Christi to Laredo as Cortez continued to twist and turn through the countryside on the mare, trying to hide his trail. Search parties kept in touch with each other by telephone and telegraph. "To ride through such a network of organized pursuit required a remarkable rider and a remarkable horse," says Paredes. "Cortez and the little brown mare were well matched for the job, as the men who pursued them testified."

When Cortez talked about the ride in later years, he gave the mare credit for helping him elude the posses—not only with her speed but also with her alertness. So sleep-deprived and exhausted that he could hardly stay in the saddle, Cortez would stop and roll himself a cigarette to try to stay awake, but the mare remained vigilant. Speaking in English, he said:

> We twist roun' in the chaparral and I am so sleep that I near fall off. I stop by one mesquite tree and make 'nother cigarette. My head he will not stand up and I fall down on that tree. Then I feel the reins jerk and when I wake up I see the ears of that leetle mare pointing where she is looking back. Far away I hear brush break and a dog bark. We go on. We cross rock hills and leave no trail, but mens are everywhere. In the day times I watch, watch and the leetle mare she is watch too. We slip tru more brush.
>
> The time would come, however, when "that leetle mare can go no more." Cortez unsaddled her and turned her loose. He patted her on the side and said, "You are one good leetle mare. Adios, my frien'."

At this point, Cortez could "go no more" either. Tired, sleepy, and weak from lack of food, he sat down in a thicket and waited for the posse to come. Two hours passed. No posse. With a little rest, his will to survive returned and spurred him onward toward the Rio Grande. Having "regained some of his strength and self-confidence," he walked, in broad daylight, into the town of Cotulla. He gambled that all of the men in the vicinity would be "out scouring brush and hills for him, guarding bridges and pasture gates," so "the safest place for him was in the towns, where they were not." He hoped he would look "like any ranchero walking into town," but his clothes were tattered, and he looked like the exhausted man he was. A Mexican woman gave him food and water when he stopped by her house, and he went below a bridge to bathe in the Nueces River, even though the bridge was guarded by men on the lookout for him. Still undetected, he crossed to the other side of the river and rested for a while before following the railroad tracks into the town of Twohig. A posse had just left, headed east. A woman in town said they were looking for a man who looked like him and warned him to "get away quick." Too tired to go very far, Cortez lay down under a water tank on the outskirts of Twohig and slept for thirty-six hours.

The posses, meanwhile, realized they had missed him at Cotulla, although they found the brown mare and recognized the tracks made by Cortez's worn, broken shoes. They began tracking him again, but, as the *San Antonio Express* reported, "owing to the many circuitous routes made by Cortez and his success in almost completely wiping out his tracks, very slow progress was made." Some of the posse members were ready to give up and go home, believing Cortez had somehow made it across the Rio Grande and disappeared.

Cortez awoke from his long sleep on the morning of his birthday, June 22, 1901. He was twenty-six. He walked into El Sauz, a little ranching village, and bought a new shirt and pair of trousers. His change amounted to $1.50 in American money; he exchanged it for Mexican currency and set out to cover the final thirty miles of his journey to the border. The countryside would be full of Mexican laborers walking from job to job on sheep and cattle ranches or in the coal mines in the area. Cortez hoped to be inconspicuous in their midst until he reached the Rio Grande and crossed over into Mexico. As Paredes points out, laborers from Mexico "crossed [the river] more or less at will in those days before stringent immigration regulations."

Cortez made it close to the north shore of the Rio Grande, not far from Laredo, but no farther. Even though many Mexicans had helped him along his way, one would betray him: Jesús González, sometimes called *El Teco* because he was from Bustamente, Mexico, home of a tribe of Indians by that name. Later those who sympathized with Cortez called González *Bocon,* or Bigmouth. He knew Cortez and recognized him when Cortez arrived at the sheep camp of Abrán de la Garza. González also knew about the one-thousand-dollar reward offered by the governor, the citizens of Karnes, and others. A party of Texas Rangers was having lunch only two hundred yards from the sheep camp when González approached and offered to lead the Rangers to Cortez. The Ranger captain, J. H. Rogers, and one other man went with González, and, minutes later, Cortez was under arrest. No shots were fired. Expecting resistance from the man who had already killed two sheriffs, the Rangers, according to William Sterling, found instead that Cortez "had reached the limit of his almost superhuman endurance, and was asleep." His *morral,* a coarsely woven bag in which he carried two pistols, was hanging in a huisache tree. Sterling says, "Cortez was awakened from his troubled sleep by a prodding Winchester in the hands of Captain Rogers." In his own words, Cortez explained, "I cannot walk more. I find ole house and nobody there. I fall on floor and I am sleep when I hear, 'Hands up.'"

For ten days he had eluded hundreds of peace officers and their deputized posses. Sterling says Cortez had crisscrossed eight counties as he traveled hundreds of miles—more than one hundred miles on foot and almost four hundred miles on horseback. At times he was being pursued by as many as three hundred men during one of the largest manhunts in history. "Most of the riders changed their mounts several times and the number of horses used in the campaign probably exceeded a thousand."

For over three and a half years after his arrest, Cortez would be held in a succession of eleven county jails and prosecuted for murdering three persons and stealing a horse. By Charles L. Convis's count, "the total number of trials reached eight." Cortez's first trial was July 24, 1901, in Gonzales for the murder of Constable Schnabel, who had almost certainly been shot by one of his fellow possemen in the shoot-out at Ottine. Nevertheless, Cortez was found guilty on a charge of second-degree murder and sentenced to fifty years in prison. On August 11, while Cortez was still in the Gonzales jail, a mob of three hundred men or more attempted to take him out and lynch him. The sheriff thwarted the attempt. Meanwhile, two days earlier, Gregorio's brother Romaldo, wounded by Sheriff Morris back in June, died in the Karnes City jail.

Cortez's second trial followed in Karnes City on October 7–11, 1901, for the murder of Sheriff Morris. This time Cortez was found guilty and sentenced to death. On January 15, 1902, the Texas Court of Criminal Appeals questioned the evidence and reversed the Gonzales verdict carrying the fifty-year sentence. Still Cortez was a condemned man facing the gallows until the Court of Criminal Appeals reversed that verdict too "on the grounds of prejudice." Before the case moved first to Goliad and then to Wharton County, "a quick and sloppy trial" in Pleasanton resulted in another guilty verdict for Cortez and a two-year sentence for horse theft. That too was overturned by the Court of Criminal Appeals. Jurors in the Goliad trial could not agree: Seven were for first-degree murder; four wanted second-degree murder; and one voted for acquittal. In Wharton County the judge dismissed the case for want of jurisdiction. Finally, the trial moved to Corpus Christi on April 25–30, 1904, and there Cortez was found not guilty of murdering Sheriff Morris. A jury of Anglo-American farmers agreed with the defense's claim that Cortez had shot the sheriff in self-defense and in defense of his brother.

The final trial was in Columbus, where Cortez was found guilty of murdering Sheriff Glover and sentenced to life in the Texas State Penitentiary in Huntsville. On appeal, the Court of Criminal Appeals upheld the conviction. Cortez entered prison on January 1, 1905. He worked as a barber and, over time, gained the respect of prison officials. The warden wrote to the governor, saying he "would like very much to see this man pardoned," and pardoned Cortez was. Governor O. B. Colquitt signed papers on July 7, 1913, granting him not a full pardon but a conditional one. It was enough to set him free. He was thirty-eight years old and had spent a third of his life in prison, all because, as Convis says, "he had traded a mare for a horse and the interpreter didn't know the difference."

Cortez settled first in Nuevo Laredo on the Mexican side of the border and joined the forces supporting Victoriano Huerta during the Mexican Revolution. He was wounded and returned to Texas, where he lived first in Manor and then in Anson, north of Abilene. He died, probably of pneumonia, in Anson in 1916 at the home of a friend. He was forty-one years old. He was buried in a small cemetery eight miles from Anson.

Along the border a ballad, or *corrido,* was written and performed "by an unknown *guitarrero*" as Cortez's "drama was unfolding." According to Juan Carlos Rodriguez:

Between Cortez's capture and his sentencing, from 1901 to 1905, the corrido *grew increasingly popular and could be heard on ranches, in bars, and at public gatherings throughout the Southwest. In at least a few cases along the Texas side of the border, singers sometimes were arrested, beaten, or even lost their jobs if they performed it in public.*

Variants of the ballad appeared in different areas as the story of *Gregorio Cortez y su yequita trigueña,* Gregorio Cortez and his little brown mare, became part of border folklore, uniting Mexicans and Mexican Americans. The *corrido* has some twenty or more verses.

As a postscript, Sterling provides information about what happened to the mare after Cortez set her free and a pursuing posse caught up with her. She was

brought to the shipping pens at Atlee. Officials of the I. & G. N. Railroad recognized the tremendous interest that the case had created among the people served by their line and transported her free of charge to San Antonio. She was placed on exhibition at the International Fair, where hundreds of curious people paid two bits apiece to see her.

Once returned to her owners, the James M. Allen family, the now famous animal was renamed Fanny Cortez.

CHAPTER TWELVE

Miriam Amanda "Ma" Ferguson
First Woman Governor of Texas

In 1917 James Edward Ferguson was impeached as governor of Texas during his second term in office, and his wife, Miriam Amanda, supervised the move from the governor's mansion in Austin to their home in Temple. That was her role, as she saw it: taking care of her husband and their two daughters. Others regarded her in that light as well, and many called her "Ma," also recognizing the coincidence of her initials, M. A.

Born in Bell County in 1875, she was influenced early on by her parents, Joseph and Eliza Wallace, and their lifestyle, and that influence guided her choices up to a point. Biographers May Nelson Paulissen and Carl McQueary observe that she "would eventually imitate in her life the domesticity she witnessed between her mother and father; she would give her children the tender care and luxuries that she felt were showered on her." As a child she had a black nurse who schooled her on the proprieties of being a real Southern lady. But an additional influence came into her life when she met and married Jim Ferguson.

Actually, she had known or known of Ferguson since he was born. A familiar story around the area was the one about his birth announcement: Jim's father, a circuit-riding preacher, had announced and prophesied at a Methodist conference in Salado, "We have named the baby Jim. He weighs thirteen pounds, and someday he will be governor of Texas." And, sure enough, he would be, and so would his wife.

Meanwhile, as a young man, Jim came courting Miriam, once she was back home in Belton after studying at Salado College and Baylor Female College. She was not particularly interested in getting married, especially to a poor Methodist preacher's son with a

Miriam Amanda "Ma" Ferguson: First Woman Governor of Texas
COURTESY STATE PRESERVATION BOARD, AUSTIN, TEXAS. CHA 1989.2,
PHOTOGRAPHER: ERIC BEGGS, 2000, POST-CONSERVATION

reputation for a hot temper. Still, he was a handsome fellow who had been all the way to California and back and could tell long and, to Miriam, amazing stories about his travels. And he was ambitious. He read law and passed his bar examination in March of 1897. He was twenty-seven; she was twenty-two. She first said no to his proposal of marriage, but his persistence paid off, and they married on the last day of the nineteenth century, December 31, 1899.

Miriam followed her domestic bent, taking care of Jim and, eventually, their two daughters. Jim became a successful banker and businessman in Temple. Then his ambitions led him into politics, and within fifteen years, he had fulfilled his father's prophecy and gotten himself elected governor of Texas in 1914. Miriam accepted her new role as First Lady and set up housekeeping in Austin.

During Jim's first term in office, he created no significant enemies and was reelected in 1916. His troubles started in his second term when he battled the University of Texas officials over the proposed dismissal of the new president and several professors. Jim, citing his own personal objections, wanted them fired; the UT president, Robert E. Vinson, understandably refused and "called for an end to political interference in educational matters." Jim retaliated by vetoing the entire state budgetary appropriation for the university. Vinson and influential UT alumni called on the state legislature to deal with Jim's "gubernatorial tyranny and one-man rule." The Speaker of the House of Representatives issued a call for a special session, a power only the governor has. Jim made the mistake of authorizing the session and found himself faced with impeachment on the basis of twenty-one charges voted by the House.

First, the House said, the UT appropriation veto was unconstitutional, but there were also charges that the governor had "illegally funneled state funds to his own purposes," had personally profited by having illegally deposited state funds in his own bank in Temple, and had accepted a bribe or illegal loan or contribution from brewing interests in exchange for his stand against Prohibition. The House called for the Senate to find the governor guilty. In an effort to escape judgment, Jim resigned. Hours later, however, on September 25, 1917, the Senate went ahead to find him guilty of several of the impeachment charges, ordered his removal from office, and barred him from ever again holding state office.

Miriam, stung by this blow to her family's name, nevertheless kept her customary low profile, and not much was heard from the Fergusons until the 1920s. That's when Jim, who had failed in his repeated efforts to get the Texas Supreme Court to declare his impeachment and ban from office unconstitutional, came up with another way to get a Ferguson in office. Miriam would run for governor. Having only minor political involvement during her husband's terms in office and certainly having no political aspirations of her own, Miriam was at first reluctant to be a part of Jim's scheme, but she finally saw her candidacy as a way to clear her family's name. Her daughter Dorrace would say later, "When Daddy asked Mama to run for governor, I suppose she just thought she had to." Dorrace's older sister, Ouida, agreed: "Always eager to help her Jim, Mamma was easily convinced that this was the thing to do."

Typically, public appearances during the campaign would follow this pattern: Miriam would speak first, according to Maisie Paulissen, "asking the mothers, sisters, and wives of Texas to help her clear her family's name." She would describe herself as "an ordinary home-loving wife and mother and grandmother" who knew little about running a government and ended with an assurance that she would seek the advice of "others." Her concluding words, often, were, "A vote for me is a vote for my husband, who cannot be a candidate." Then Jim could get up and promise voters they would get "two governors for the price of one." He also told them, "If God's in his heaven and a Ferguson is in the Governor's Mansion, all's bound to be right with Texas."

In spite of her genteel upbringing and her education, Miriam allowed herself to be portrayed during the campaign as a sunbonnet-wearing country girl, plain and simple. Other Texas women began wearing sunbonnets too in a show of solidarity. Jim would have campaign bands strike up "Put on Your Old Gray Bonnet." A popular campaign slogan was "Me for Ma, and I ain't got a durned thing against Pa." Daughter Ouida later wrote that she would never call her mother "Ma" because "it didn't fit her dignity."

Miriam's chief opponent in the 1924 Democratic primary was Judge Felix Robertson of Dallas. He had the support of the Ku Klux Klan in Texas, and the Ferguson-run campaign was not only against Robertson but against the Klan itself. That led to other slogans such as "the sunbonnet pitted against the hood" or "a petticoat against a bedsheet." The Fergusons claimed Robertson was nothing more than a puppet of Klan Wizard Hiram W. Evans, a Dallas dentist. Jim called Evans the "Grand Gizzard." Nevertheless, Robertson won the first primary, but Miriam beat him in the runoff. In addition to her anti-Klan stance, she said she was against state spending and the current prison system and that she wanted to improve highways. As the Democratic nominee in a predominantly Democratic state, at that time, she easily defeated the Republican candidate, George C. Butte, a former dean of the University of Texas law school. Butte had predicted that Miriam's victory would bring "a government by proxy" to Texas and would lead to "the greatest example of irresponsible personal government that history records."

For the moment, however, her election was historic simply because she became the first woman governor of Texas, and this only four years after women in the United States got the rights to vote and to hold public office. She was actually the first woman in the United States to be elected governor, but only the second inaugurated. Wyoming's Nellie T. Ross, fulfilling her late husband's unexpired term, was inaugurated fifteen days earlier. When the Fergusons once again drove up to the Governor's Mansion in January 1925, Miriam reputedly said, "Well, we have returned! We departed in disgrace; we now return in glory!" Phase one of their vindication was achieved.

The new governor wasted no time proposing an amnesty bill that would allow Jim to hold state office once again and make the vindication complete. The legislature passed it, and she signed it into law in March of 1925, although later its validity would be challenged by Attorney General Dan Moody. Another significant piece of legislation during Miriam's first term was the passage of an anti-mask bill aimed at eradicating the Ku Klux Klan by exposing its members. It was later overturned by the courts. She then took on other goals outlined in her campaign: "a general reduction in state expenditures, a general lowering of taxes, stricter regulations of interest rates, sound administration of penitentiaries, more aid to county schools and less aid to 'high brow' institutions." Still, she was careful not to antagonize officials at the University of Texas. She had learned from Jim's experience the lesson about their potential to wreck a governorship.

But she hadn't learned the lessons, apparently, about the additional scheming that had contributed to Jim's impeachment. From the start, Jim had a desk in the governor's office right beside hers, and he was quick to offer "advice and counsel." During the campaign he had said, "Don't worry I'll be there to chop the wood and carry in the water!" He added, "I'll be around to give her a hand." The evidence is strong that he handed her advice that very nearly got her impeached, and she was foolish enough to take it.

Rupert Richardson writes: "During the second era of Fergusonism (1925–27), reform took a holiday." That era, of course, marked Miriam's first term. Initially there was the matter of pardons and paroles from state prison. Having promised both in her campaign and in her first message to the legislature that she would adopt a "most liberal" pardon policy, she approved the release of 239 convicts in the first seventy days of her administration. The number had topped a thousand before the end of 1925 and reached a total of 3,595 by the end of her two-year term. On average, she pardoned one hundred convicts per month. The press was keeping score, and some of Miriam's critics suggested that the pardons were bought and paid for by the friends or families of the prisoners. Jokes and stories began to circulate. One, aimed at Jim, described a father driving to the Fergusons' farm in Bosque County to see if Jim couldn't use his influence with the governor to get the man's son out of prison. Jim allegedly pointed to an old swayback horse—or sometimes it is a mule—and asked the man if he didn't want to buy it for $150—or sometimes up to five thousand dollars. When the man asked why he'd want to be thinking about a horse at a time like this, Jim would reply, "Well, if you bought it, your son could ride home from prison on it."

Another joke made light of Miriam's pardoning policies. That story had the governor visiting Rice University in Houston or maybe riding on an elevator at the state capitol. When a man jostled her or accidentally stepped on her foot, he said, "Oh, madam, please pardon me." Her response was, "You will have to see my husband about that."

So were the Fergusons selling pardons, as many believed? Two secretaries have told different stories. Gladys Little, secretary to the governor, said that supplicants did bring "sentimental little gifts" like patchwork quilts and a small handcrafted wooden house with perforations in it that spelled out "Home Sweet Home" when it was lighted from the inside. Nola Wood, who processed the pardons through the attorney general's office, however, said the Fergusons accepted "cold cash" and put it in a basket marked "personal."

Miriam, of course, justified her policies on loftier grounds. She observed that a high percentage of those in prison had been convicted of Prohibition laws. They were poor people, often members of a minority race, imprisoned and therefore unable to work and support their families, "while wealthy Texans violated the laws at will and even drank imported liquors at the private clubs in Galveston, Houston, or San Antonio." More than eight hundred of the pardons she issued during her two-year term went to Prohibition violators.

In addition to the pardoning rumors, Governor Miriam was also accused of loading state agencies with "friends of the family" and of setting her husband up as a member of the Texas State Highway Commission where he could receive kickbacks on contracts, bribe officials, and engage in profit-sharing through ownership of a company that did business with the state. He could also urge companies bidding for contracts to advertise in the Ferguson newspaper, *The Forum*. As these accusations spread, and because many in state government still believed Miriam was no more than a puppet governor whose strings were being pulled by her husband, some politicians once again called for a special session, hoping to impeach her. Remembering the mistake Jim had made in 1917 by authorizing a special session, she refused to make a similar error.

Even though she had dodged impeachment, allegations of wrongdoing continued to circulate. Two of the three highway commissioners resigned; there were rumors of mismanagement in the state prison system and in textbook commissions. Miriam's reputation had been damaged enough that she was defeated in her bid for a second term by Dan Moody, former attorney general. One of Moody's first acts in office was to repeal the law that would have allowed Jim Ferguson to hold a state office. Miriam was still eligible, though, and she ran again in 1930, losing in a primary runoff to oilman Ross Sterling. She ran again in 1932. This time she beat Sterling, who was probably as much a "casualty of the depression" as he was done in by the Ferguson campaign. A big businessman himself, the former president of Humble Oil and Refining Company, he seemed to be "poorly equipped philosophically to be governor in a time of crisis," according to Donald W. Whisenhunt. Miriam took office in January 1933 in the midst of the Great Depression and faced the challenges it brought.

To her credit, she acted responsibly as the state's leader during the worst of economic times. When banks began to fail nationally, she quickly closed Texas banks for three days—for "Texas Independence Week," she said—to prevent a run. She also took advantage of federal New Deal programs such as the Federal Emergency Relief Administration, Civilian Conservation Corps, National Youth Administration, and Works Progress Administration designed to help people who had lost their jobs. Estimates are that these programs provided temporary employment for about a fourth of the state's population during her second term. Although both she and her husband were teetotalers, she supported the repeal of Prohibition, arguing that it had been a failure and simply encouraged the illegal sale of alcohol, "bootlegging," which made some people rich.

During her second term she continued to issue a great many pardons to convicts, and she and Jim were again accused of accepting money for the clemencies. She could not escape persistent charges of graft and scandal, at least from some quarters, and was accused of using the Texas Highway Department as "a source of patronage for her political supporters." By this time "Fergusonism" had become a familiar term to Texas voters, but, as Rupert Richardson points out, it meant "different things to different people. . . . Critics angrily denounced the Fergusons as unprincipled demagogues, but to their loyal supporters, they were undaunted crusaders seeking justice for the oppressed."

Totaling her two terms as governor and Jim's one and a half, Miriam said that seven years in office were "honor enough for one family" and declined to be a candidate in the 1934 election, a race she likely could have won. She did run again, unsuccessfully, in 1940, but then retired permanently to private life. Jim died in 1944, and she continued to live quietly at her home in Austin, where her chief hobby was tending her garden. Although she stayed interested in politics, she seldom actively campaigned for anyone, the exception being Lyndon Baines Johnson. From the time he made his first bid for a congressional seat through the Kennedy-Johnson presidential campaign in 1960, she was a Johnson supporter.

Reflecting in later years on what she considered to be her own list of accomplishments, she cited aid to "education, mental health, welfare, and the improvement of working conditions for laboring people." She continued to argue that she and Jim were just "common folk," avoiding any demonstration of "conspicuous consumption" and living modestly. She said they had always ridden "in open Model T's when campaigning since Pa thought sedans looked plutocratic." Summing up her reasons for wanting to be governor of Texas, she said one remained paramount: "of course, everyone knows that my main incentive was to clear away the cloud that political hatred had draped about the honorable name of Ferguson. I wanted to right the grievous wrong which enmity had perpetrated upon my husband, James E. Ferguson, once Governor of Texas. Frankly that was my reason of reasons for seeking office."

How successful she was at righting that wrong and to what degree the Fergusons were opportunists, schemers, or downright scoundrels is still subject to some debate. In Norman D. Brown's assessment, "In the murky world of statute books, there may well have been no illegality, but the Fergusons were guilty of a flagrant abuse of the ethical standards of public office." Whatever her own impulses may have been, most historians still see Miriam as Jim's proxy in office, and, clearly, as Billy M. Jones suggests, "their careers were truly as inseparable as were their personal lives together. A remarkable couple indeed! And they more or less dominated politics in Texas for almost three decades—at least they were the most talked about actors on the Texas political stage from 1914 to 1940."

Before Miriam died on June 25, 1961, at the age of eighty-six, she did have her share of honors, one of which came on Mother's Day in 1953. The Texas Senate approved a special resolution, citing her not as a strong political leader but as "an example of noble and gentle womanhood, an ideal wife, and a devoted mother." A couple of years later, over three hundred people gathered at the Driskill Hotel in Austin to honor her on her eightieth birthday. One of the guests was "a grateful Lyndon Baines Johnson." Those present serenaded her, harking back to her 1924 campaign song, "Put on Your Old Gray Bonnet."

She is buried alongside "her Jim" in the Texas State Cemetery in Austin.

CHAPTER THIRTEEN

H. L. Hunt
Oil Tycoon

There was once a Texas oilman who would occasionally introduce himself to strangers by saying, "Hello, I'm H. L. Hunt, the world's richest man." At the time, he was making no idle boast. An April 1948 issue of *Life* magazine published a photograph of Hunt and, under the photograph, posed this question: "Is this the richest man in the U.S.?" Its sister publication, *Fortune,* attempted an answer, saying that Hunt was "the biggest of The Big Rich, and thus also probably the richest individual in the U.S." Bryan Burrough, author of *The Big Rich,* says both magazines underestimated Hunt's net worth at $237 million at a time when "it was probably closer to $600 million." Throughout the next two decades Hunt was still hailed as the richest man in the country, some said the richest in the world, although Burrough says "he almost certainly wasn't." Still, he was certainly in the top ten. By the time he died in 1974, his fortune was estimated at between two and three billion dollars. He was earning about one million dollars a week.

Not bad for a fellow who started off working on his father's farm in Illinois, had no formal education to speak of, and ran away from home at sixteen to travel across the United States working as a dishwasher, farmhand, cowboy, lumberjack, and muleskinner. His road to wealth began when, at age twenty-two, he inherited between five thousand and six thousand dollars after his father died in 1911. Hunt invested that money in a 960-acre cotton farm near Lake Valley, Arkansas, in the Mississippi Delta. Ambitious to do something more than farming, however, he began to speculate in cotton and timberland in Louisiana and accumulated some fifteen thousand acres in Arkansas and Louisiana by 1920.

H. L. Hunt: Oil Tycoon
AP PHOTO/ANTHONY CAMERANO

During World War I he'd been smart enough to grow cotton on his own land while cotton prices were high, but after the war the cotton market collapsed. The value of his land plummeted as well, so he looked for other sources of income. That's when he got in the oil business. He heard about an oil strike in El Dorado, Arkansas, and headed that direction. He traded in oil leases until he had enough money to lease a half acre of his own. He brought in an old rotary drilling rig, drilled, and struck oil. Soon he owned forty-four producing wells in the area. In 1924 he sold a half interest in forty of those wells for six hundred thousand dollars, a hundred times more than the small inheritance he'd started investing with thirteen years earlier.

Like many successful entrepreneurs, Hunt was a risk taker and, in his case, an outright gambler. During the 1920s he continued to speculate in oil ventures and in real estate booms in Arkansas, Louisiana, and Florida, and he continued to play cards. Even without a formal education, Hunt was something of a prodigy as both a reader and a mathematician and had begun playing card games as a young child. While on the road as a teenage runaway, he played poker and other card games—and won. When any of his business ventures left him land rich but cash poor, he turned to gambling. He played cards in Arkansas and downriver in New Orleans, where the stakes were higher.

Biographer Ardis Burst cites one example of his gambling success in New Orleans, when he began playing with one hundred dollars worth of chips in a high-stakes poker game, added six hundred dollars to his holdings by the time he took a supper break, and returned to sit in on a no-limit game to parlay his winnings to $10,200 by midnight. He always quit playing at midnight. Even though he was matched up with some of the most famous professional poker players in the country, he said he could win because "he knew more about them than they knew about him." At that, he considered himself enough of a professional at one point to adopt a moniker for himself: Arizona Slim. He kept that nickname for the rest of his life.

His other nickname was June or Junie, short for Junior. He was born Haroldson Lafayette Hunt Jr. in 1889, the youngest of eight children. He likely inherited something of his entrepreneurial bent from his father, known as Hash, a farmer and dealer in farm products and agricultural futures. From his mother, Ella, a former teacher, June received his early education before homeschooling was a common practice. The only time he went to the grade school was to play "three-cornered cat" ball games during the noon hour. Hunt would say later, "There was no reason for me to attend public schools, since my elder brothers and sisters had brought home the Primer and the First, Second, Third, Fourth, and Fifth Readers, and my mother was the wisest and smartest person and the best teacher I ever knew." His older siblings claimed June could read aloud from newspapers by the age of three. Others marveled at his mathematical skills; as a child he could multiply large sums in his head. Part of his prowess with numbers he could no doubt attribute to his photographic memory. According to biographer Harry Hurt, June had a particularly good memory for cards. "After only a brief glance at an upturned deck, he could then name each card in sequence almost without error." That skill would stand him in good stead with his later poker playing.

Even without any kind of public school degree (he had taken the elementary finishing examination at age nine and was second only to his brother Leonard, who was two years older and had gone to public school), June talked his way into Valparaiso University in Indiana not long after he'd left home at sixteen. There he studied Latin, algebra, rhetoric, zoology, and history for two semesters and stood second in his class before a severe case of tonsillitis forced him to drop out. He never went back. The rest of his education came through experience and trial and error.

He believed in what he called "Hunt Luck." One of his favorite sayings was "Given the choice between luck and intelligence, always take luck." So even though in both his gambling and his business interests he would certainly hedge his bets, do the math, and study the odds, in the end his decisions were often intuitive, based on what his son Ray later called his "sixth sense." Burst explains it this way: "Like a painter who creates masterpieces without being able to explain his philosophy of art or a great scientist whose discoveries stemmed from following his 'hunches,' Hunt put together pieces in a way he could not explain and followed rules he could not teach to anyone else." James Presley points out that Hunt often spoke of "creating" great wealth. Presley interprets the claim to creativity as "the feeling of magic engendered by the discovery of oil." Where there was nothing, he says, "suddenly there is something valuable which has been 'created' by 'magic.'"

Hunt continued to operate on hunches and to follow up on tips, including one he got in 1930 from M. M. Miller, an El Dorado oil equipment entrepreneur. "There's a wildcatter working down in east Texas," Miller said, "and he may have something going." That wildcatter was seventy-year-old Columbus M. "Dad" Joiner, who had discovered a vein of oil on his four-thousand-acre lease in Rusk County, but he was broke and had oversold interests in the well. He couldn't raise the capital to drill. Hunt had very little cash himself, but he used thirty thousand dollars invested by an El Dorado clothier plus the promise of an additional $1.2 million payout from expected oil revenues to buy out Joiner. Thus Hunt acquired rights to a sizable portion of one of the greatest oil discoveries in the world up to that time, and it would be the cornerstone of his own fortune.

As he took his place as one of the Big Rich in Texas, he was publicly regarded as a very wealthy eccentric who wore off-the-rack suits, drove an ordinary sedan, carried his lunch to the office every day in a brown paper bag, and mowed his own lawn once a week. Yet, in many ways, his opinion of himself was rather grandiose, and he believed he carried a "genius gene." Perhaps that, plus an allegedly powerful libido, accounted for his being the father of fifteen children with three women in his lifetime. According to Harry Hurt, "He believed that by fathering children he was doing the world a favor, providing the human race with its future leaders, even as he provided himself with an ever-increasing flock of self-images." What the world would not know until after his death was that Hunt was a bigamist.

Wife number one was Lyda Bunker, a former teacher with a family lineage she could trace back to William the Conqueror. Hunt married her in Arkansas on November 26, 1914, when they were both twenty-five. They had seven children, one of whom died as an infant. During their early married years in Arkansas, Hunt seemed to settle into family life and was frequently seen taking his wife and children to the movies on the weekends. In reality, however, he was often gone from home on business. That pattern changed somewhat when the family moved to Tyler, Texas, in 1931, in part because he spent six months laid up with a back injury and in part because his east Texas oil field interests were close by. "The time we lived in Tyler," he would say later, "may have been some of the best days we had as a family."

By 1938 Hunt's base of operations was Dallas, and he moved his family there in January of that year. He bought a house north of downtown on White Rock Lake. Designed as a replica of George Washington's home in Virginia, the Dallas Mount Vernon sat on ten acres, and Hunt even bought deer to give the place more of a country feel. Lyda joined the Dallas Women's Club, the Daughters of the American Revolution, and the Highland Park Presbyterian Church. The *Dallas News* reported that "quite the nicest family has come to Mt. Vernon Dallas to stay." What Lyda would soon discover, however, is that her husband had a second family living in Houston and that another woman was claiming to be his wife.

Wife number two was Frania Tye (probably short for Tiburski). Introducing himself as Major Franklin Hunt, he married her in Florida on Armistice Day, November 11, 1925, or, at least, Frania thought he did. They had met when he went to Florida to consider buying some real estate, and he began to court her. Good Catholic that she was, she would have no part of an extramarital affair, so he arranged for them to be married by a justice of the peace in Tampa's Cuban quarter, although he produced no marriage license at the time. Any other documents confirming that the union took place were missing or inconclusive as well, as later investigations revealed. Now living a double life, Hunt was a frequently absent husband to Frania in Shreveport, Louisiana, until 1930 and then in Dallas until 1934, when she discovered his real name and his other marriage. In all, Hunt fathered seven children between 1926 and 1934, four with Frania and three with Lyda.

When Frania acted on her own suspicions, after reports from others, and confronted Hunt in 1934, he admitted that he was not Franklin but rather H. L. and that he was, in fact, married to Lyda. He then moved Frania, pregnant with their fourth child, from Dallas to Great Neck, New York. According to Burst, even after his confession, he "was apparently unwilling to abandon his relationship with Frania or to alter his relationship with the children." He bought Frania a house in an estate section of Great Neck and continued to provide generous financial support. He poured out his feelings for her in prose and poetry. In one telegram to her he said he was en route to see her because "too strong the urging, / my engine is surging." At one point he asked her to become a Mormon because it was a religion in which "having two or three wives was normal." She refused.

Still Frania went along with some of Hunt's less extreme plans, one of which was to move her from New York to Houston in 1939. By now she was using the name Mrs. H. L. Hunt, and she began an active social life in Houston. That ended rather abruptly, however, when she began getting telephone calls from a woman who threatened to expose Frania as Hunt's "mistress or something to that effect." Refusing to be blackmailed, Frania once again confronted Hunt, demanding some kind of resolution. She wanted to meet Lyda and finally did, declaring her "the finest woman I ever met." Recognizing now that any satisfactory reconciliation with Hunt was not going to happen, Frania reached a financial agreement with him in 1942 and signed papers swearing they had never been legally married. Twelve days later she married John W. Lee, a Hunt Oil employee.

Meanwhile, Hunt had taken up with the woman who would become wife number three: Ruth Ray, a onetime secretary in the offices of Hunt Oil Company in Shreveport. She was two years younger than Hunt's oldest daughter. Their relationship began in 1942, and he moved her to Dallas less than two years later where she took the assumed name of "Wright." Unlike Frania, Ruth did know about Hunt's first wife and family from the beginning and accepted her role as Hunt's well-kept mistress until after Lyda died. Then she began to take what she thought was her rightful place by Hunt's side, spending much of her time at Mount Vernon and pressuring Hunt to marry her. Marry her he did in Dallas on November 24, 1957, two years after Lyda's death in 1955. He adopted her four children, born between 1943 and 1950, who were, of course, actually his.

Hunt died November 29, 1974, at age eighty-five. In his obituaries, his conservative political views got more notice from the press than his great wealth. The *New York Times* labeled him "a militant anti-Communist . . . and ultraconservative." And that was true. Since the early 1950s he had increasingly turned his attention to conservative causes and ideals, founding the *Facts Forum* in 1951 as an "educational foundation." Later he founded *Life Line,* producing fifteen-minute radio programs. In 1952 he headed an effort to get General Douglas MacArthur to run for president and only reluctantly agreed to support Eisenhower. That same year *Facts Forum* endorsed Senator Joseph McCarthy, the junior senator from Wisconsin who became chairman of the House Un-American Activities Committee and promised to ferret out Communist "infiltrators."

Hunt's office was just around the corner from the Texas School Book Depository where the alleged assassin of John F. Kennedy set up his sniper's nest and fired the fatal shots at the president in 1963. Because Hunt had been a vocal critic of Kennedy and his policies, an FBI agent advised Hunt to get out of town following the assassination. When, two days after the assassination, police arrested Jack Ruby for shooting Lee Harvey Oswald, Kennedy's accused killer, they found copies of two *Life Line* scripts in Ruby's coat pocket. Burrough says Ruby had been "outraged" by the radio attacks on Kennedy. Editorial writers across the country said *Life Line* at least contributed to the "climate of hate" in Texas. Hunt received death threats, his phone ringing sometimes in the middle of the night. "At one point, someone even fired shots at Mount Vernon." Federal investigators targeted Hunt for a time, and H. L., Bunker, and Lamar were all mentioned in the Warren Commission's report. All were cleared of any wrongdoing or "any substantive ties to either Oswald or Ruby." Still Hunt's reputation as a "right-wing maniac" and an "anti-Communist nut" followed him to the grave.

Some of the obituaries, however, were not so quick to pigeonhole Hunt for his political leanings only and recognized his complexities. One *Texas Monthly* writer described him as "many men in one, multitudinous and contradictory." Hunt was buried beside his first wife, Lyda, in Dallas's Hillcrest Memorial Park. Then the real stories began to emerge about Hunt's secret personal life.

Frania and her children had not been mentioned, much less provided for, in Hunt's will, so within a year she began legal action against the estate. The case would not make its way to court in Shreveport until January of 1978. A Shreveport newspaper sensed the drama the revelations were likely to generate and began a three-part series of articles: "Haroldson Lafayette Hunt, the late Texas oil billionaire, maintained the wife of a bigamous marriage in Shreveport for years in the 1920s." On the first day of the trial, Ray, Ruth's son and executor of Hunt's estate, said that he was "of the impression that H. L. Hunt is the father of [Frania's] children." Still, although it was determined that a marriage license had likely been issued, there was no documentation that a wedding had actually taken place. Nevertheless, the Hunt lawyers began negotiating for an out-of-court settlement. In a head-to-head meeting between Ray and Frania in the judge's chambers, a final arrangement granted Frania $7.5 million, half of Hunt's estimated community property in 1942 when he and Frania made their final break.

During the course of the trial, reporters from all over the country converged on Shreveport and gave the story front-page coverage. On the third day of the proceedings, Frania took the stand and described in great detail the history of her relationship with Hunt. According to Burst, Frania "did not condemn Hunt in her testimony, but reiterated that she had loved him and that she had tried to do her best to balance her feelings for him with the needs of their children." When questioned about her swearing to the 1942 statement that omitted any mention of marriage, she answered, "Yes, I swore, but I signed that statement to protect Mr. Hunt from a bigamy charge. That was my contribution to his life."

It is Harry Hurt's opinion that "Hunt was not ashamed of his secret lives and secret families. On the contrary, he was proud of his ability to support more than one wife and family, and he was proud of his exploits at the gambling tables." Furthermore, it is likely, according to several of his biographers and at least one of his daughters, that Hunt did not confine his philandering to Frania Tye and Ruth Ray. In the 1980s his daughter June spoke about his infidelity and indicated that she was aware of his continuing relationships with women other than her mother, Ruth. "He did not see himself as having to go by the ethics of—anything. In fact, that is how he acted. In any area, I think, though he would not use this phrase, it was as though he was a god unto himself who could make his own rules. And the end justified the means." Even Lyda seemed, in a way, to excuse her husband's behavior. After she found out about Frania, Lyda told her daughter Margaret, "Daddy always said that his genes were so outstanding that he wanted to leave a lot of them to the world. I am certain that he does not imagine there is anything the matter with this. He is so naïve."

For all his womanizing and gene distribution, however, Hunt did seem capable of love, if not monogamous commitment. He was apparently devastated when Lyda suffered a stroke in 1955, at the age of sixty-six. As Burrough observes, "Despite the other women in his life, Lyda had been Hunt's rock." Returning on the plane from the Mayo Clinic, where she died, Hunt wept. "I don't know how I'll ever get by without her," he said. He more or less disappeared for six months on a tour of Latin America. When he returned, Burrough says, "it was the love of his mistress, Ruth Ray Wright, and his secret 'third' family" that saved him. For her he even gave up gambling and embraced religion, joining the Dallas Baptist Church.

Oilman, bigamist, Christian conservative—he was all these things and more. And perhaps it was his "wildcatter's" independence, his need to call the shots and take charge, that led to his greatest successes and his greatest failures as a man. As the *Texas Monthly* writer said, Hunt was certainly "many men in one, multitudinous and contradictory."

CHAPTER FOURTEEN
George B. Parr
The Duke of Duval

Lyndon Johnson once described George Berham Parr as "the man that casts more Democratic votes than anybody else in the state." And LBJ should know as Parr likely delivered the votes that led to Johnson's election to the US Senate in 1948.

Parr inherited his status as kingmaker in south Texas from his father, Archer Parr, better known as Archie. Archie Parr, a third-grade school dropout born on Matagorda Island in Calhoun County, had moved to Duval County in 1882 at age twenty-two. He had worked as a horse wrangler, ranch hand, trail boss, and ranch manager until he could finally acquire land of his own near Benavides in the southern part of Duval County. By the early 1900s he began to forge the political empire to which his son fell heir.

It was common practice among the Anglo-American and European-born landholders and business owners in south Texas, and certainly in Duval County, to use their economic dominance to exploit their Hispanic workers. So although Mexican Americans made up the great majority of the population—outnumbering Anglos two to one—their voting was managed and manipulated, generally through coercion and intimidation, by the *jefes,* the bosses. Archie Parr added patronage to the mix and set up his own feudal fiefdom, he as *patrón* taking care of his *peones*. According to Evan Anders, Parr "professed concern for the welfare of the Hispanic laborers and small-time farmers and stockmen" and "offered more than coercion as an incentive for supporting his campaigns." He learned Spanish and looked after the special needs of his workers, paying for weddings and funerals and providing relief during hard times. He saw to it that some Mexican Americans had a shot at upward mobility by getting them county jobs and occa-

George B. Parr: The Duke of Duval
1975 *CORPUS CHRISTI CALLER-TIMES.* REPRINTED WITH PERMISSION.

sionally offering them cash disbursements of questionable legality from county coffers. One county official described the arrangement as "frankly corrupt but fully benevolent." In return Parr expected loyalty, extending to the ballot box. With the support of his Mexican-American constituency, he got himself elected county commissioner and, eventually, state senator.

By this time, Parr was married and had five children, one of whom was George, born in 1901 in San Diego, the county seat, located fifty-two miles west of Corpus Christi. At age thirteen, George served as his father's page in the Texas Senate and began to learn the ways and means of using and abusing political power. In the late 1920s he began managing local affairs in Duval County as Archie's attention turned more and more to state and national matters. When his father died in 1942, George took over the entire political machine Archie had built and surpassed Archie in the role of *El Patrón*.

George Parr became even more fluent in Spanish than his father, made an effort to learn the names of his Mexican-American constituents and their children, and continued to provide help in times of need. He too expected absolute loyalty in return. Although he served as county judge and county sheriff at various times, he had no particular ambitions to hold office himself, but he did intend to stay the undisputed political boss of Duval County. The press began calling him the Duke of Duval.

Meanwhile, the Duke had experienced what could have been setbacks when he was convicted of income tax evasion in 1934 and even had to serve a nine-month prison term in 1936 and 1937 for parole violations. Still his favored candidates continued to sweep county elections with there being no apparent damage to his political power. He had managed to amass a sizable fortune as well with income from banking, ranching, oil, and other business interests—with a likely dip into the public treasury too, on occasion. According to Robert Dalleck, the Duke "made his fortune through the manipulation of county contracts and on the backs of unskilled Mexicans earning $16 a week." Nevertheless, Parr was pardoned for his misdeeds by

President Harry Truman in 1946 and regained his own right to vote as he persisted in manipulating the votes of others.

Then came the elections of 1948 and his most notorious scheme of all.

Three men were vying to be the Democratic candidate for US senator from Texas: Houston attorney George Peddy, former governor Coke Stevenson, and Congressman Lyndon Baines Johnson. In the first primary vote in July, Stevenson had the most votes but not the required majority, so he and Johnson were thrown into a runoff. Both stumped the state. Johnson even rented a helicopter he dubbed the "Flying Windmill" and drew curious crowds each time it landed on fairgrounds or in the middle of rural pastures. And both men, or their supporters, curried favor with political bosses in various regions of the state, especially in south Texas, where boss rule was strongest.

The August heat wore on as Johnson and Stevenson campaigned for the Democratic Party's nomination, knowing that the winner of the primary would surely take the general election in November as well. Texas was a one-party state in 1948, and that party was Democratic.

On the day of the primary runoff vote, August 28, Stevenson held a statewide lead and was the apparent winner. The Johnson forces rallied supporters and called on party bosses. Apparently George Parr answered the call. Although Parr had supported Stevenson for governor, he had now switched allegiances because Stevenson had crossed him. Five years earlier, in 1943, Parr and others had advised then Governor Stevenson to appoint their man, E. James ("Jimmy") Kazin, to the recently vacated post of Laredo District Attorney in Webb County, and Stevenson had the audacity to choose another man instead. That wouldn't do at all, and Parr told Stevenson so. When Stevenson asked for his help in the Senate race, Parr reportedly said, "Coke, you know we can't support you." In fact, he added, "we're going to have to be all out against you." He expected loyalty from his elected officials too, and, as Dallek observes, Parr was committed to "no ideology, except the survival of his machine." He, therefore, "favored and opposed politicians according to his needs."

Parr had already guaranteed Johnson a landslide runoff victory in Duval County and Starr County, where he had the most influence. Initially, in his home county, Parr had delivered 4,195 votes for Johnson and only thirty-eight for Stevenson, more than one hundred to one plurality. But when the call for more votes came in, Parr would do more. Since Parr and his men "just counted 'em" the way they wanted, they waited to see how many more votes they needed to deliver. Almost a million votes had been cast statewide in the runoff, most of them on paper ballots. Precinct judges unfolded the ballots and called out the name of the candidate receiving the vote on Election Day while clerks recorded the tally on three separate lists. The precinct judges then reported the totals to the Texas Election Bureau by telephone or telegraph. Mistakes were to be expected during the counting, copying, tabulating, and reporting since the votes might pass through the hands of as many as eight groups. So corrections in the days following the actual vote were not uncommon.

Parr's election officials told the Texas Election Bureau that the returns from one of the Duval County precincts had not yet been counted. This announcement came more than twelve hours after the polls closed. Parr's power was such that the only limit to the number of votes he could report would be the number of poll taxes he had paid.

Since 1902 in Texas payment of a poll tax had been a requirement for voting. It had come into being in a number of states as a means of disenfranchising African Americans, Native Americans, Mexican Americans, and poor whites and wouldn't be abolished until 1964 when the Twenty-fourth Amendment to the US Constitution was ratified. Parr and other south Texas bosses generously paid the poll taxes for their Mexican-American county inhabitants and then told them how to vote. They voted for Johnson in the primary and in the runoff, but Johnson still needed more.

More than twenty-four hours after the polls closed, Duval County officials reported 427 previously unreported votes from that "uncounted" precinct, two for Stevenson, 425 for Johnson. As Johnson biographer Robert Caro points out, "4,662 persons thus voted in a county in which only 4,679 poll tax receipts had been issued—the 99.6 percent turnout was an astonishing display of civic responsibility." Another "corrected" return from the Rio Grande Valley netted eighty additional votes for Johnson from Starr County. But even that wasn't enough. Although these "corrections" gave Johnson the lead briefly, additional rechecking from other counties brought Stevenson's totals back up so that he was several hundred votes ahead.

Once he had exhausted possibilities in Duval and Starr, Parr finally had to look to the east, to neighboring Jim Wells County, to defeat Stevenson and elect Johnson. Although Parr had less power there, he had enough to pressure those who did wield power: Ed Lloyd, the local boss, and Luis Salas, the election judge for Box Thirteen, the poorest Mexican-American district in Alice, the Jim Wells County seat.

Salas was Parr's enforcer in Jim Wells County. A big man—six-foot-one, 210 pounds—he was called "Indio" because of his swarthy appearance. His physical strength, combined with his savage temper, made him a man to be feared among the local population. As a recipient of Parr's largesse, Salas was intensely loyal, for through Parr's influence Salas had achieved status as a badge-wearing, gun-toting law enforcement official. At one time a city policeman in Alice, he also served terms as deputy sheriff in Duval, Jim Wells, and Nueces Counties. He had a car; he had money; and he had Parr's orders. In later years Salas would acknowledge, "In all these years, George told me to give our candidates 80 percent of the total votes, regardless if the people voted against us." No problem, he added. "I had control of most of the Mexican Americans in the county; they voted the way I tell them to vote." And if they didn't? No matter. The Parr candidate would get 80 percent anyway because, as presiding election judge in Box Thirteen, Salas would be the one "counting" the ballots.

In 1948 Salas had already done his job during the first primary vote on July 24. In a vacant lot across from the polling place in Nayer Elementary School in Alice, Salas arranged for a large tent to be erected. Armed deputy sheriffs stood guard at the front of the tent. Other deputies rounded up Mexican-American voters and herded them into the tent to receive their poll-tax receipts. They were also given sample ballots and their instructions. Salas said it was necessary "to teach some of our voters how to vote; lots of them needed training." He got out the vote during the runoff election as well.

Tuesday, at 7 p.m., seventy-two hours after the August 28 election, was the deadline for precinct election judges to turn over to their county chairmen all ballot boxes. These were to contain not only the actual ballots but the tally and poll sheets as well. That was the Texas election law. But Parr made his own laws in the counties that made up his domain. Friday morning, six days after the election, forty-five more votes for Johnson came in from Zapata County. Additional corrections from across the state, some of them no doubt legitimate, had reduced Stevenson's lead to 157 votes.

Recalling Parr's instructions—"Listen, Indio, concentrate on the senatorial race. Be sure we elect Johnson."—Salas responded when Parr told him to add two hundred votes to Johnson's total in Jim Wells precinct thirteen by using the names of people from the poll-tax list there who had not voted. Salas gave the job to two of his aides, who added two hundred votes for Johnson and only one for Stevenson six days after the polls had closed. In their haste, the aides listed the additions in alphabetical order and wrote the names in a different color ink from those on the legitimate voting list. If, as the law required, they made three copies of the poll lists and tally sheets, all three from Box Thirteen mysteriously disappeared after the final "corrected" tallies were reported to the Texas Election Bureau. Salas would testify later that the two copies of the lists he had in his car must have been stolen while he was in a tavern drinking beer. The third list was supposed to be in the ballot box, but when a judge later opened the box, it had only ballots, each signed on the back by Salas, but no lists. So even though some of the Democratic county officials in Jim

Wells County and three others had seen at least one poll list long enough to copy some of the names and to note that the names after voter number 841 ran in alphabetical order, without the originals there was no concrete evidence of fraud.

In Duval County, meanwhile, the actual ballots from the August 28 runoff had been burned by the courthouse janitor within six weeks of the runoff and before the general election. Reportedly the Johnson camp had asked that no ballots be destroyed since it would reflect badly on Johnson. Parr is supposed to have replied, "To hell with you. I'm going to protect my friends."

Before the tally sheets and poll lists disappeared entirely, Stevenson and two of his attorneys were able to look at the ones Tom Donald, secretary of Jim Wells County's Democratic Executive Committee, had in his desk at the Texas State Bank in Alice—the bank owned by George Parr. Donald quickly took them away when the attorneys began copying names. The two men nevertheless managed to memorize enough additional names to create a list of alleged last-minute voters to question. Several signed affidavits saying they had not voted in the runoff election.

As if to counter any accusations Stevenson might offer, Johnson reminded the press that corrected totals coming in from a west-central county and a couple of Gulf coast counties had given Stevenson 338 more votes. "I'm sure that all of the mistakes have been honest mistakes," Johnson said, "but nevertheless, Stevenson has been kept in the running by those mistakes."

Stevenson's challenges notwithstanding, it was ultimately left to the sixty-two-member Democratic State Executive Committee to certify the candidate. The vote of those present was close, twenty-nine to twenty-eight for certifying Johnson as the party's candidate. Then one woman withdrew her vote for Johnson and abstained, producing a twenty-eight to twenty-eight tie. The chairman hesitated to break the tie without calling the roll of delegates one more time. At the last minute, a delegate from Amarillo, rumored to be hauled out of a hotel bathroom, entered the room and cast the deciding vote to certify Johnson.

So the plus two hundred votes from Box Thirteen had netted Johnson an eighty-seven-vote winning margin in the primary runoff, and a hunted-down delegate had given him a one-vote victory in the Democratic State Executive Committee. The press dubbed Johnson "Landslide Lyndon," a label Johnson would embrace with self-deprecating humor in speeches and interviews throughout the rest of his political career. And, although he never admitted to having any knowledge of the probable voter fraud in south Texas, he frequently told a joke about a little Mexican-American boy who was sitting on a curb in Alice crying. "Son, are you hurt?" asked a passerby. "No, I no hurt," the boy replied. "Are you sick?" "No, I no sick." "Well, are you hungry?" "No, I no hungry." "Then what's the matter? Why are you crying?" the passerby asked. "Well, yesterday, my papa—he's been dead four years—yesterday, he come back and voted for Lyndon Johnson, didn't come by to say hello to me." In fact, Dudley Lynch points out that at least three names on the Box Thirteen poll list were of people who "had been dead for years."

Even though manipulated bloc voting was not uncommon in Texas politics at the time, Caro concludes that the "one-sided votes which were decisive in Johnson's victory were cast at the direction of a single man who, moreover, did not have to 'vote 'em' but simply to 'count 'em.'" Both the size of the Parr-delivered vote in 1948 and the timing of the delivery meant that Parr "could decide the result of any close statewide election." A September 27, 1948, *Time* magazine article described him as "a powerful kingmaker" and credited him with being "the man most responsible for Congressman Lyndon Johnson's nomination over Coke Stevenson for the U. S. Senate." But the battle, in this case, was not quite over.

At Stevenson's urging a federal injunction to keep Johnson's name off the ballot followed as did a federal district court hearing in Fort Worth and federal master-in-chancery investigative hearings in Alice and San Diego. Parr's powers were severely limited in this new setting, but he kept a close eye on the proceedings in south Texas while Johnson's attorneys worked to get the injunction lifted. Meanwhile, despite testimony to the contrary, Salas denied, under oath, any wrongdoing. At length, Supreme Court Justice Hugo Black ruled that a federal judge should not be meddling in a state election. The injunction was lifted; the hearing was over; and Johnson's name was placed on the ballot. He easily defeated Republican Jack Porter in the November election and took his seat in the Senate.

In later years an attorney asked Tom Miller, mayor of Austin and a Johnson supporter, who really won the 1948 election. Miller replied, "They were stealin' votes in east Texas. . . . We were stealin' votes in south Texas. Only Jesus Christ could say who actually won it."

Although never in so dramatic a fashion as in 1948, Parr would continue to get out the vote for Democratic candidates. A *Time* magazine article published at the time of Parr's death in 1975 observed that he had maintained his "well-greased machine" and that "Duval County went for Kennedy and Johnson by a 12 to 1 margin in 1960, and John Connally, vying for the gubernatorial nomination two years later, swept the county 14 to 1." In fact, only once between 1916 and 1972 did the Democratic candidate receive less than 74 percent of the vote in Duval County. That was in 1956 when a mere 68 percent voted Democratic. A number of times the Parr machine delivered over 90 percent, including the 97 percent in 1948.

Parr did not fare so well in his personal and business life, however. He was implicated, although never indicted, in at least one politically motivated murder and was convicted of threatening a Jim Wells County restaurant owner with a gun and fined one hundred dollars. Another conviction was for using the mails to defraud a school district of $220,000 by issuing checks to nonexistent people. Once again he failed to pay his federal income taxes—this time amounting to more than one million dollars—and had to declare bankruptcy. And yet again, in 1974, the government went after him for failing to report $287,000 in income, and he was sentenced to five years in prison. He posted bond and began an appeal.

When Parr failed to appear for a court date on March 31, 1975, a team of deputies, state police, and FBI agents went looking for him. They found him the next morning, April 1, on his ranch, Los Harcones. He was at the edge of a pasture slumped over the steering wheel of his 1969 Chrysler Imperial, a bullet in his brain.

Not even his suicide, however, and the collapse of his organization brought political bossism to an end in south Texas. The family network has continued to be influential in the county. As evidence, perhaps, Duval County has remained one of the strongest and most consistently Democratic localities in Texas, still frequently giving candidates more than 70 percent of the vote. In the 1988 and 1992 presidential elections 82 percent of the county's voters cast ballots for the Democratic candidate. In 2008, Democratic presidential candidate Barack Obama received 74.8 percent of the county's vote.

There's no hint that these more recent Democratic victories are the result of old-style bossism, however. It's not likely, in this day of electronic voting machines, that election fraud on a grand scale is even possible, meaning that the Box Thirteen episode in 1948 was destined to "become part of our national folklore," as John E. Clark puts it. In Clark's estimation, it "put Parr in the big league of political bossism and election chicanery with such Hall of Shamers as Boston's James Michael Curley, Chicago's Richard J. Daley, and the likes of Boss Crump of Memphis, the Pendergast machine of Kansas City, and Boss Tweed and the Tammany Hall gang in old New York." A dubious distinction, indeed.

CHAPTER FIFTEEN

Bonnie Parker
Outlaw Partner

You've read the story of Jesse James
Of how he lived and died.
If you're still in need
Of something to read,
Here's the story of Bonnie and Clyde.

So begins a poem titled "The Trail's End," written by Bonnie Parker. It continues for fifteen more stanzas, finally concluding, "Some day they'll go down together / they'll bury them side by side. / To few it'll be grief, / to the law a relief / but it's death for Bonnie and Clyde." They did "go down together" in 1934 in a hail of lawmen's bullets fired from an ambush near Sailes, Louisiana, but their story begins in Texas.

Bonnie Parker and Clyde Barrow met in January of 1930 in Dallas. She was nineteen; so was he, if his March 24, 1910, birth date recorded in the Barrow family Bible is correct. Other sources say he was born in 1909. One version of their meeting says that Parker was out of work and staying at the home of a neighbor or friend. Another says she was doing housework for the neighbor. Biographer Jeff Guinn says she went to a party at the house of her brother and sister-in-law. All versions have Barrow stopping by as a visitor or guest, and he and Parker were immediately smitten with each other—although she was already married.

Bonnie Elizabeth Parker was born October 1, 1910, in Rowena, Texas, near San Angelo. Her father, a brick mason, died when she was four, and her mother moved her and her two siblings to Cement City, an industrial suburb of Dallas. Parker was a good student, winning top prizes in spelling, writing, and public speaking. She was attractive and popular, and she fell for a good-looking, smart-

Bonnie Parker: Outlaw Partner
WESTERN HISTORY COLLECTIONS AT THE UNIVERSITY OF OKLAHOMA

dressing classmate named Roy Thornton, who already had a police record for burglary. They got married six days before her sixteenth birthday in 1926. Although they never divorced, in reality their marriage was short-lived. Thornton would disappear for long periods of time, without explanation. Bonnie began working as a waitress in Dallas and wouldn't take Thornton back when he showed up one last time in January of 1929. She never saw him again but continued to wear her wedding ring.

Bonnie and Clyde's first romantic interlude was brief as, about three months after they met, Clyde was sentenced to fourteen years at Eastham Prison Farm in April of 1930 for having cracked safes, robbed stores, and stolen cars. These were not his first convictions. He had a police record dating back to 1926 when he was only sixteen. Paroled from Eastham in February of 1932, Barrow returned to Dallas to rekindle his affair with Bonnie, and the two embarked on a two-year crime spree that would lead to their violent deaths.

They teamed up with Ralph Fults, a man Barrow had served time with at Eastham, and began a series of small robberies, mostly of stores and gas stations. On April 19, 1932, Bonnie and Fults were captured and jailed following a failed hardware store burglary in Kaufman, Texas. Although the county grand jury declined to indict her, Bonnie was not released from jail until June 17. In the interim she whiled away her time by writing poetry. Within weeks of her release, she reunited with Barrow.

By early 1933 Barrow and his gang had murdered five people during robberies or getaways, but it wasn't until April of that year that Bonnie and Clyde gained notoriety nationwide. The two of them, plus Clyde's brother Buck and his wife, Blanche, and a young gang member named W. D. Jones, were hiding out in an apartment in Joplin, Missouri. The fivesome created suspicions among the neighbors by being loud and generally indiscreet as they drank beer and played cards late into the night. At least one neighbor called the police. Five lawmen responded in two cars, thinking they might be confronting a bunch of bootleggers in the apartment. Bent on escape, Clyde, Buck, and Jones fired on the officers, killing one instantly and fatally wounding another. They bundled Bonnie in the car and pulled Blanche in off the street as she chased her fleeing dog. In the melee, Buck was grazed by a ricocheting bullet, Jones was hit in the side, and Clyde was struck but unhurt as his suitcoat button deflected the bullet. The gang got away, but they left most of their possessions behind.

Among those possessions were several rolls of film and one of Bonnie's handwritten poems. The local newspaper, *The Joplin Globe,* developed the film and printed photographs of Bonnie, Clyde, and Jones clowning around with weapons pointed at each other and of Bonnie, a pistol in her hand and a cigar in her mouth with her foot up on the front bumper of a car. The newspaper also published Bonnie's poem titled "The Story of 'Suicide Sal'" ; it recounted the sad tale of a woman taking the rap for a man she loved who abandoned her once she was imprisoned. Sal says, "If he had returned to me sometime, / Though he hadn't a cent to give / I'd forget all the hell that he's caused me, / And love him as long as I lived." The romantic poem and the photos went out on the newly installed newswire and made front-page news all across the country.

The group kept moving and robbing all the way from Texas to Indiana and Minnesota. In several instances they kidnapped lawmen or robbery victims and later released them, sometimes giving them money to help them get home. Tales of these encounters made headlines, too, increasing the folkloric stature of the outlaws. In other instances members of the Barrow Gang did not hesitate to shoot and kill lawmen or civilians whom they saw as a threat to their freedom. Law enforcement authorities stepped up their pursuit.

On June 10, 1933, Clyde Barrow was driving with Parker and Jones near Wellington, in the Texas Panhandle. With no barricades or signs to warn him that a bridge was out, Clyde rolled their car into a ravine. In the wreck Parker received third-degree burns on her right leg, as well as serious burns on her arm, face, and chest, when the car caught fire. They got help from a nearby farm family, rendezvoused with Buck and Blanche Barrow, and made it to a tourist court near Fort Smith, Arkansas, to hide out and give Bonnie some time to heal, but a botched robbery and the murder of a town marshal by Jones and Buck Barrow in Alma, Arkansas, soon had them on the run again.

Their next close encounter with the law came in July just south of Platte City, Missouri, where they had rented both cabins at the Red Crown Tourist Court. Nearby was the Red Crown Tavern, a bar and restaurant popular with Missouri Highway Patrolmen. Owner Neal Houser became suspicious of the group, especially when his guests taped newspapers over the windows of the cabins. He alerted one of his restaurant patrons, Captain William Baxter of the Highway Patrol. The town druggist aired his suspicions too when Clyde and Jones came in to buy bandages and atrophine sulphate to treat Bonnie's leg. He alerted Sheriff Holt Coffey. The sheriff consulted with Captain Baxter, and Baxter called for reinforcements from Kansas City. Coffey led the assault on the cabins, he and his fellow officers armed with submachine guns. They were no match for the firepower of Clyde's Browning automatic rifles, and the gang members shot their way out and escaped once more.

This time there was one really serious casualty, however. Buck Barrows had sustained a horrific head wound that left him little hope for survival. His wife, Blanche, was almost blinded with glass fragments in her eyes. The group stopped to camp near Dexter, Iowa. By now the manhunt for the Barrow gang was well publicized, and local citizens in Iowa alerted authorities to the likelihood that the wounded strangers camped at Dexter Park might be the fugitives. Local lawmen and about one hundred spectators surrounded the campsite, and the gang was once again under fire. Buck was shot again, this time in the back, and he and Blanche were captured. The others escaped on foot. Buck died five days later.

Now there were three: Clyde Barrow, Bonnie Parker, and W. D. Jones. Their faces on wanted posters all over the country, they stayed on the run—west to Colorado, north to Minnesota, southeast to Mississippi—trying to keep a low profile. Yet Barrow and Jones still pulled small robberies for expense money, and they restocked their arsenal by burglarizing an armory in Plattesville, Illinois, in late August.

They risked going back to Dallas in early September so Bonnie's and Clyde's families could help attend to Bonnie's medical needs. The burns on her leg were so severe that the muscles contracted and caused the leg to "draw up." Once in Dallas, Jones left them and went to Houston, where his mother lived. So now there were two.

Word of Bonnie and Clyde's whereabouts led the Dallas sheriff to set a trap for them on November 22, 1933, as they attempted to meet up with family members near Sowers, Texas. Barrow sensed the danger as he approached, however, and drove right past his family's car. The sheriff and his deputies stood and fired their submachine guns and a Browning automatic rifle. No family members were hit, but a BAR slug penetrated the getaway car, hitting both Barrow and Parker in the legs.

Now so badly crippled she could barely get around, Parker nevertheless accompanied Barrow when, in January of 1934, he finally made good on his vow to seek revenge on the Texas Department of Corrections—a vow he'd made following the harsh treatment he'd received at Eastham Prison Farm. In a brazen move Barrow orchestrated the escape from Eastham of several prisoners, including Raymond Hamilton and Henry Methvin. One of the escaping prisoners shot a prison officer, and this act prompted the Texas and federal governments to step up their manhunt for Barrow and Parker even more. The Texas Department of Corrections brought in former Texas Ranger Captain Frank A. Hamer to hunt down and bring to justice or kill Bonnie and Clyde.

On Easter Sunday in 1934, an eyewitness, who was later discredited, claimed Barrow and Parker killed two young highway patrolmen near Grapevine, Texas. Barrow did shoot one of the men, but it was prison escapee Methvin who shot the other. The eyewitness reported that Bonnie not only shot one of the patrolmen but also laughed as she did so. With that image spread throughout the country through news coverage, whatever romantic fascination the general public may have had with Bonnie and Clyde was replaced with a clamor for their capture or extermination. The Highway Patrol and the Texas governor's office offered rewards for the two, dead or alive. Public hostility increased when less than a week later Barrow and Methvin killed an Oklahoma constable. Hamer continued to study Bonnie and Clyde's habits and haunts and began to shadow them from place to place.

He and a posse made up of four law enforcement officers from Texas and two from Louisiana set up an ambush on May 23, 1934, on a rural road in Bienville Parish, Louisiana. They were armed with pistols, shotguns, and Browning automatic rifles. Just after nine o'clock in the morning, Bonnie and Clyde appeared on the road in a stolen light gray Ford V8 sedan. Clyde slowed the car as they approached his "mailbox"—a drop under a board by a tree stump where his associates could leave messages. Hamer said he called out, "Throw up your hands!" When the two were not quick to "stick 'em up," Hamer and his men opened fire, emptying the automatic rifles, then the shotguns, then the pistols. The parish coroner counted seventeen bullet holes in Barrow's body and twenty-six in Parker's. The two did "go down together," but they were not buried side by side. Parker is buried in the Crown Hill (or Fishtrap) Cemetery and Barrow in Western Heights Cemetery, both in Dallas.

The fascination with the pair did not end with their deaths. If anything, it increased. Newspaper and magazine articles, books, and movies purported to tell the "real story" of Bonnie and Clyde or to so romanticize them that the public would be understandably confused about what they did and why. About Bonnie, in particular, the questions remain about why she stayed with Clyde and just how involved she was in the crimes he committed, especially the murders. C. F. Eckhardt claims she pulled a pistol or her "sawed-off twenty-gauge automatic shotgun" on several occasions. Conversely, John Neal Phillips says that even Barrow's prison mate and onetime gang member Ralph Fults "could never understand her attraction to the outlaw life. She hated guns and rarely participated directly in any crime." Yet, Fults said, she "felt somehow shut out, inferior." She confided in him once, "I'm just a loser—like Clyde. Folks like us haven't got a chance."

Apparently the devotion she felt for Barrow bordered on obsession. "It didn't matter what he had done," Phillips says; "she was prepared to follow him all the way to the penitentiary if necessary." She followed him farther than that, as it turned out, and even predicted their likely violent end. She wrote it into "The Trail's End" poem and seemed resigned to accept Clyde's vow "to die rather than contribute to a society that seemed intent on keeping an ex-con from earning an honest wage." It must be said, however, that even Clyde himself tried, on more than one occasion, to get Bonnie to give herself up and avoid the same fate he anticipated for himself. She refused, saying, "When my time comes, I want to be with you." Ted Hinton, one of the men on Bonnie and Clyde's trail, had told Clyde's father that "no one in the world would be happier than I if Clyde and Bonnie would come in [and surrender]. I'd given my word that if they ever did decide to give up the chase, I'd guarantee their safety until they had a fair trial." Hinton suggested to Clyde's parents that "there was always a possibility that a jury might give Bonnie a break, and, for all I knew, maybe a good lawyer could help even Clyde beat the [electric] chair."

Hinton had been acquainted with Bonnie even before she met Clyde. She had been working as a waitress in a restaurant in Dallas where Hinton took his meals. He liked her and thought her pretty "with taffy-colored hair that glistened red in the sun and with a complexion that was fair and tended to freckle." He spoke of "the sparkle she had when I knew her, when she was waiting tables." As a Dallas deputy, Hinton was one of the officers on the ambush stakeout in Louisiana and fired his own weapons into the death car. His images of Bonnie seem to blur and merge as he describes opening the door on Bonnie's side of the car after the shooting was over, saying the impression would stay with him forever: "I see her falling out of the opened door, a beautiful and petite young girl who is soft and warm, with hair carefully fixed, and I smell a light perfume against the burned-cordite smell of gunpowder, the sweet and unreal smell of blood."

Mixed images of Bonnie abound in accounts written about her during and since her time spent with Clyde Barrow. Some picture her as a sweet young innocent who simply got mixed up with the wrong man. That can't be entirely true, certainly, as she'd already been drawn to and married a man given to criminal pursuits and destined to spend time in prison himself.

Others go to the other extreme and cast her as a hardened criminal in her own right. H. Gordon Frost and John H. Jenkins claim that Frank Hamer told a friend that Bonnie "was cleverer [than Clyde] and equally merciless in the matter of taking human life without provocation of any sort. She loved whiskey and kept herself stimulated with it. She couldn't carry it well, however. Every time she got too much her legs gave out. She couldn't walk. Clyde had to carry her to their car many times." Jeff Guinn explains that although Bonnie did drink, her inability to walk was the result of "the terrible leg burns she'd suffered" in the car wreck near Wellington. She "could no longer stand by herself" and "mostly hopped rather than walked." Clyde had to hold her up or carry her. Guinn also says, "Bonnie didn't mind having guns around. She just didn't want to shoot them."

The widely circulated photograph of her with a pistol on her hip and a cigar in her mouth prompted the label "cigar-smoking gun moll," one Bonnie hated and tried to dispel. Hinton went beyond saying the photograph was nothing more than her little joke and insisted that the photographer who developed the film left behind in Joplin, Missouri, altered it by actually drawing in a cigar as a joke of his own making. Hinton claimed that in the original Bonnie held a rose in her mouth. Whether the cigar was real or penned in, Bonnie wanted it known that she didn't smoke it or any other. Percy Boyd, one of the people Bonnie and Clyde kidnapped and later let go, said he talked quite a bit with Bonnie during his ride with them and that she asked him to tell people the truth. "She said she didn't want her public to think of her as a girl who smoked cigars, because nice girls don't smoke cigars. She was pretty mad about it."

She did have her "public," judging from the number of people who showed up at her funeral—probably fewer than the twenty thousand her mother estimated, but still thousands. In her own way, Bonnie was very ambitious and apparently longed to be regarded as a "nice" girl, in spite of her life choices. She told Hinton "she'd have liked being a singer, or maybe a poet, and she used to sing when she was in school at Cement City, west of Dallas." She continued to write poetry, even while in jail or on the run. But her fame came not from her artistry but from her loyalty to a man considered by some to be "public enemy number one" in an era of other notable public enemies with names like "Pretty Boy" Floyd, "Machine Gun" Kelly, John Dillinger, and Al Capone. From the start, Bonnie's loyalty to Barrow was absolute. She first proved it not long after they met when, in March of 1930, she smuggled a loaded revolver to Clyde while he was being held in the McClennan County Jail in Waco, Texas. He subsequently broke out of jail and escaped to Illinois.

Although several films about Parker and Barrow have been released since their sensational deaths, it's the 1967 film *Bonnie and Clyde* that "made movie history," as Web Maddox points out. A low-budget "sleeper" movie produced by Warren Beatty, who starred in it with Faye Dunaway, it "is probably among the all-time leaders in gross profits." More romanticized than factual, it nevertheless depicts Bonnie and Clyde as rebels, "the foremost practitioners of protest in their day, supreme activists one might say." Its theme and, for the day, rather explicit sex scenes got both the critics' and the moviegoing public's attention. Maddox says, "With motion pictures now considered an art form, it would please Bonnie and Clyde mightily to know that they contributed to a conspicuous trend in contemporary culture." Bonnie for sure might appreciate knowing her life eventually became the basis for art.

CHAPTER SIXTEEN
Madalyn Murray O'Hair
Political Activist

Madalyn Murray came to Texas in 1965 for the second time and promptly got herself arrested. She and her younger son, Jon Garth, arrived in San Antonio on September 25 after she had been deported from Mexico. She was wanted in Maryland for assault and battery against the police. It was a dramatic entrance into the state.

Drama was nothing new for Murray. She had already been labeled "the most hated woman in America" in a 1964 *Life* magazine article. Her notoriety stemmed chiefly from her having filed a lawsuit, *Murray v. Curlett,* in 1960 against the Baltimore, Maryland, City Public School System, in which she asserted that it was unconstitutional for her older son, William, to be required to participate in Bible readings at Baltimore public schools. In time her lawsuit was consolidated with another, *Abington School District v. Schempp,* and reached the Supreme Court of the United States in 1963. The Court ruled eight to one in Murray's favor, which effectively banned coercive prayer and Bible verse recitation at public schools in the United States.

She added to her unpopularity in October 1963, when, on behalf of her newly formed Freethought Society, she had her attorney, Leonard Kerpelman, sue to eliminate the city of Baltimore's church tax exemptions. The public was outraged, and the Catholic Archdiocese of Baltimore was worried enough to immediately contest the suit. It was still ongoing when Murray came to Texas.

None of that had any direct bearing on her being arrested in San Antonio, however. Her scuffle with the police in Baltimore had been about a runaway girl whose parents wanted her back. Susan Abramovitz, a seventeen-year-old schoolgirl, had taken up with Bill Murray,

Madalyn Murray O'Hair: Political Activist
AUSTIN HISTORY CENTER

Madalyn's older son. Susan's father did not approve of the courtship. Susan ran away from home and showed up at the Murrays' house in March 1964. Madalyn claimed the girl had "a black eye and a swollen nose and a piece chipped off her tooth and swollen mouth and bruised breasts. . . ." Bill later said his mother exaggerated the injuries but did admit that Susan's father had hit her. After briefly moving back home, Susan disappeared again and this time went to Niagara Falls with Bill. They weren't married, and she was underage.

Susan's parents filed a complaint in criminal court, suing Bill for "causing a minor to be without proper guardianship" and for taking Susan out of Maryland. A judge signed a restraining order directing Bill and Madalyn to keep away from Susan and placed Susan in the custody of an aunt and uncle.

Madalyn, meanwhile, arranged for the young couple to be married and go away for their honeymoon, in flagrant violation of the restraining order. So the police continued to look for them and were waiting at Madalyn's house when Bill and Susan returned. Madalyn managed to get Susan in her car and drive her to another location then returned to do battle with the police. A witness, Lemoin Cree, said, "She became very wild," and the police were quite rough with her. She, her mother, and Bill were arrested. Madalyn was charged with kicking an officer and threatening two more with a tear gas pen; Bill was charged with hitting two officers to keep them from arresting Susan; and Lena, Madalyn's mother, was charged with hitting an officer. They requested jury trials and promptly made plans to flee.

Madalyn spent Bill's college fund buying tickets to Hawaii for herself, sons Bill and Garth, Susan, Lena, and Madalyn's dogs. Madalyn hired another attorney to fight their extradition back to Maryland and applied for new passports, thinking she might ultimately defect to Cuba. Sometime around Memorial Day in 1965, only Madalyn and Bill headed instead to Mexico. Later they were joined by Garth, Susan, and Robin, Bill and Susan's infant daughter.

Instead of being granted political asylum in Mexico, Madalyn was deported less than four months after her arrival. There were several versions why. One was that she was traveling with a fake passport; another was that she attempted to expose a drug ring Mexican authorities were in on; and yet another was that she had been reported as a fugitive wanted in Maryland. At any rate, she wound up in Texas, and there she stayed.

In early October, Madalyn's and Bill's indictments in Maryland were overturned, and there was no more threat of extradition. By this time she was in Austin, and, as biographer Ann Rowe Seaman says, "The minute she set foot there, she knew it was home." In spite of its general conservatism, Texas appealed to Madalyn because of its "deference to . . . human individuality, to human freedom."

Meanwhile, Richard O'Hair, a man Madalyn had met and fallen in love with in Mexico, arrived in Austin, and the two were married on October 18, 1965. A former Marine, O'Hair had lived in Mexico for a decade when he met Madalyn. She saw in him a creative, revolutionary, rebel hero. He had studied at the Chicago Academy of Fine Arts and was a painter—as well as a licensed private investigator. Articulate and educated, he was a good storyteller who had led an exciting life. Rumors were that he worked for the CIA, and he had been recruited, as a matter of fact, to spy for the FBI. In the 1940s he had joined the Communist Party as an infiltrator and had testified before the House Un-American Activities Committee in 1952, exposing at least sixty Communists by name. He didn't tell Madalyn that last part, as she hated the HUAC. One of O'Hair's fellow FBI informants said O'Hair's plan was to marry Madalyn, "find out her Communist connections," and "let the FBI know." If that was the case, his seduction of her was said to be simply an act of patriotism. Seaman says, however, "O'Hair may have hoped to get . . . in the FBI's good graces by cultivating Madalyn, but he came to respect and love her." Their relationship was certainly stormy at times, and they ultimately separated, but they stayed married until Richard's death in 1978.

Once settled in Austin, Madalyn founded American Atheists, described as "a nationwide movement which defends the civil rights of non-believers, works for the separation of church and state, and addresses issues of First Amendment public policy." She acted as chief executive officer. Husband Richard became president of the Society of Separationists, or SOS, Inc., the "action arm" she founded. She latched on to every opportunity to go public with her views, including an interview with *Playboy Magazine* in 1965. In that interview she said she left Baltimore not because she feared prosecution for assaulting police officers but because of persecution from Baltimore residents. She listed alleged incidents of harassment, intimidation, and even death threats against her and her family. Still she did not back off her message that religion was "a crutch" and an "irrational reliance on superstitions and supernatural nonsense."

In 1966 she published a pamphlet, "Why I Am an Atheist," in which she said, "I am a bit more than that—an Atheist. I am, in fact, the Atheist. The Atheist who made Americans stop to take a little stock of their accepted values." She continued to file lawsuits that managed to keep her in the public eye—even though most of those lawsuits failed. She went on speaking tours and was the first guest on the Phil Donahue television show in 1967 when it debuted as a local program in Dayton, Ohio. She would make several more appearances during the run of the program. Her brazen, outrageous style made her "colorful" and "good copy." It also earned her enemies, not only among Christians but among atheists as well. Even her family began to fall away. Her older son, her mother, and her brother all disassociated themselves from her at one time or another. Only Garth, the younger son, and Robin, the granddaughter she adopted, remained with her throughout.

After the three *Apollo 8* astronauts read the Genesis creation story from their Gideon Bibles on Christmas Eve in 1968 as they orbited the moon, Madalyn filed another lawsuit. One of the astronauts offered a prayer at the end of the reading. She asked the courts to ban US astronauts—government employees, after all— from public prayer in outer space. The US Supreme Court rejected the case for lack of jurisdiction.

By the end of 1969 she and Richard had established Poor Richard's Universal Life Church as a tax-exempt entity in Austin. They made Neanderthal Man the church's patron saint. Madalyn founded an atheist radio program and hosted *American Atheist Forum,* a television show carried on more than 140 cable television systems. In the early 1970s she envisioned holding yearly conventions. All these projects fueled her own personal ambitions, her view of herself as a leader. "I love a good fight," she said. "I guess fighting God and God's spokesmen is sort of the ultimate, isn't it?" She wrote in her diary in 1972 that she was sure she could change America and get rich in the process. "I want money and power and I'm going to get it," she wrote. She set goals: By age fifty-five, she wanted an expensive, well-furnished home and Cadillacs for herself and her associates. She would be wearing "a mink coat and svelte clothes." In 1974 she would run for governor of Texas, she said, and in 1976 for president of the United States. At other times she wanted to elevate her sons to power. Bill, who was in and out of her life during the 1970s, would be governor (she didn't care which state) under her O'Hair Plan, and Garth would be President of the United States by the time he was eligible at age thirty-five.

The most public voice and face of atheism in the United States during the 1960s and 1970s and into the 1980s, Madalyn continued to be, largely by design, a controversial and polarizing figure. In 1984 she wrote speeches for porn magnate Larry Flynt's presidential campaign and had written articles for Flynt's *Hustler* magazine; she was still appearing on radio and television talk shows. She tapped Jon Garth, now going by Jon only, as her successor as leader of the American Atheists. He was not well liked, and various chapters began seceding from the main group. By 1991 all the remaining local and state chapters were dissolved so that American Atheists amounted to no more than Madalyn, Jon, Robin, and just a few support personnel. Still they persisted, published, and pontificated.

In February 1993 Madalyn hired a handsome ex-con named David Waters as a typesetter and shortly thereafter promoted him to office manager. Such trust she had in him that she did not suspect him of thefts within the office, including seventy thousand dollars worth of government bearer bonds removed from an office safe. That all changed in early April 1994 when she returned from a two-week trip to California and found that American Atheists had been all but wiped out: bank accounts drained of fifty-four thousand dollars, employees laid off, bills unpaid. Waters left a message on the telephone answering machine saying that he had resigned.

In spite of Madalyn's demands, Austin police and the district attorney's office were slow to act. Only after they finally ran a thorough criminal record check on Waters did they indict him for theft on July 7, 1994. They discovered he had previous convictions for murder, forgery, assault, burglary, criminal trespass, drunk driving, and weapons charges. He'd been in and out of reform school and prison since he was a teenager. Even so, he and his attorney worked out a plea bargain very favorable to Waters. In exchange for his pleading guilty to theft, to being a habitual criminal, and to three lesser counts, he was sentenced to ten years' probation and required to make restitution. He was a free man, and Madalyn was understandably frightened. Yet she wrote a scathing article in the "Members Only" section of the American Atheists newsletter exposing Waters and his previous crimes as well as the theft in Austin. Her tell-all narrative was prompted in part by her wish to protect herself and her family by establishing a semipublic record of events and in part, no doubt, by some degree of revenge. Biographer Ted Dracos says that, after reading a copy of the newsletter,

> *Waters started having his own revenge fantasies, but they were somewhat more ambitious than Madalyn's. He wanted to first snip off her toes one by one with a bolt cutter and then murder her. Strangling would be good. But before he killed her, he would extort a fortune from her, and her children, so that he and his girlfriend could live in luxury happily ever after.*

On August 27, 1995, Madalyn, Jon, and Robin suddenly disappeared.

The door to the American Atheists office was locked with a note attached to it. The note, apparently signed by Jon, said, "The Murray O'Hair family has been called out of town on an emergency basis. We do not know how long we will be gone at the time of the writing of this memo." Inside Madalyn's home, breakfast dishes were still on the table; her diabetes medication was on the kitchen counter; and her dogs had been left behind. Phone calls from the trio a few days later claimed they were in San Antonio on business, and Jon ordered six hundred thousand dollars worth of gold coins from a San Antonio jeweler, taking delivery of only five hundred thousand.

American Atheist employees and friends reported receiving several more phone calls from Jon and Robin up until September 27. Neither explained why they left or when they might return. Some reports were that their voices sounded "strained and disturbed." Many speculated that the Murray O'Hair family had taken the money and run, perhaps to New Zealand. Another theory was that fundamentalist Christians had kidnapped the trio or that Madalyn had died of natural causes and her remains had been secretly disposed of to prevent her Christian son, Bill, from giving her a "Christian burial." One year to the day after their disappearance, Bill Murray filed a missing persons report. Madalyn, Jon, and Robin were declared legally dead, and many of their assets were sold to clear their debts.

In time, suspicions of foul play focused on David Roland Waters, the same man who had confessed to stealing thousands from American Atheists, the same man Madalyn had angered by exposing and denouncing him in her newsletter. An investigation confirmed that, in fact, Waters and his accomplices had kidnapped Madalyn, Jon, and Robin, forced them to withdraw the missing funds, gone on several huge shopping sprees, and then murdered all three. One of the accomplices, Danny Fry, was murdered as well. Waters eventually pleaded guilty to charges of kidnapping, robbery, and murder and was sentenced to twenty years in federal prison, where he died of lung cancer in 2003. In January 2001 he had led police to a burial site in a dry riverbed on a five-thousand-acre Texas ranch. There the bodies of the three missing Murray O'Hairs were unearthed. Their remains showed extensive mutilation, and identification had to be made through dental records, by DNA testing, and, in Madalyn's case, by the serial number of her prosthetic hip. Also in the mass grave were Fry's head and hands.

So Madalyn Murray O'Hair's second trip to Texas ended in her gruesome murder. Her first trip had offered a bit more promise. Born in Pittsburgh, Pennsylvania, in 1919, she was baptized a Presbyterian and reared by churchgoing parents. She spent the first thirty years of her life in Pittsburgh, in Ohio, in the military as an officer in the Women's Army Corps, and back in Ohio before moving to Texas in 1949 with her parents and her young son, William Joseph Murray III. She had married John Henry Roths in 1941, but Bill's father was a married Army officer with whom Madalyn had an affair. She later divorced Roths. In Houston Madalyn took a job as a probation officer for Harris County and earned a law degree in 1952 from South Texas School of Law. She either failed or refused to take the Texas bar examination, however, and never practiced, although she would certainly use her knowledge of law in her various dealings with the courts. She moved again with her parents, this time to Baltimore, Maryland, in the fall of 1952. There she had a second son, Jon Garth, also fathered by a man she did not marry. It was there that she started her political activism to demand secularism in schools and government.

Madalyn's son Bill was permanently estranged from his mother once he converted to Christianity on Mother's Day in 1980. He was baptized in a Baptist church in Dallas and even took up work as a preacher. Madalyn's response was to "repudiate him entirely and completely for now and all times . . . he is beyond human forgiveness." Murray said, after his mother's death, that although she certainly "did not deserve to die in the manner she did," she was nevertheless *an evil person. . . . Not for removing prayer from America's schools . . . No . . . She was just evil. She stole huge amounts of money. She misused the trust of people. She cheated children out of their parents' inheritance. She cheated on her taxes and even stole from her own organizations. She once printed up phony stock certificates on her own printing press to try to take over another atheist publishing company. I could go on but I won't.*

Others criticized her abrasive, dictatorial ways. According to author Ann Rowe Seaman, "She couldn't delegate authority, she was mean to her followers, she was unappreciative of their sacrifices. They worked for a pittance because they believed in her cause, and she would curse them and write terrible things about them and fire them."

So it isn't so much a matter of her beliefs—or unbelief—that qualifies her as a "jerk," but her behavior in general. She has been faulted for failing to address fundamental issues of ethics and morality in her own life and as they relate to those who are nonreligious, and she clashed not only with religious believers but with many atheists as well, expelling members of American Atheists who did not conform to her ideas of how they should behave. Dracos considered her a "deeply corrupt, depraved human being." In the end, in the opinion of her son Bill, "It was her love of power over people that finally caused not only her death but the deaths of my brother and my daughter." The three were buried in a common grave, and no prayers were said.

CHAPTER SEVENTEEN
Lee Harvey Oswald
Alleged Assassin

Lee Harvey Oswald said he didn't do it. The Warren Commission said he did. The House Select Committee said he did too, but that he may have had help—although committee members could never produce conclusive evidence or a specific suspect.

Meanwhile, there is plenty of convincing evidence that Oswald shot and killed President John F. Kennedy in Dallas, Texas, on November 22, 1963: For starters, he worked at the Texas School Book Depository, the building from which shots were fired, so he had opportunity. Furthermore, he owned the weapon that fired the fatal shots, although he bought it under an assumed name.

Yet he persisted in saying, after he was arrested and charged, that he was set up, that he was a patsy, although he wouldn't say by or for whom. In his hallway interviews with newspaper reporters, he claimed police brutality. He was vocal but hardly cooperative. Two days after Kennedy's assassination Oswald was shot and killed by Jack Ruby in the basement of the city jail while the whole world was watching on television. Since then commissions, committees, historians, conspiracy theorists, and others have researched and speculated, argued and postulated, and still there are differing opinions about just what the evidence proves. It would seem, as Norman Mailer concludes in *Oswald's Tale,* "Evidence, by itself, will never provide the answer to a mystery. For it is the nature of evidence to produce, sooner or later, a counterinterpretation to itself in the form of a contending expert in a court of law." So Oswald will forever remain the "alleged" assassin of President Kennedy.

Certainly most of those who were alive and alert in late November of 1963, especially those in Texas, can remember where they

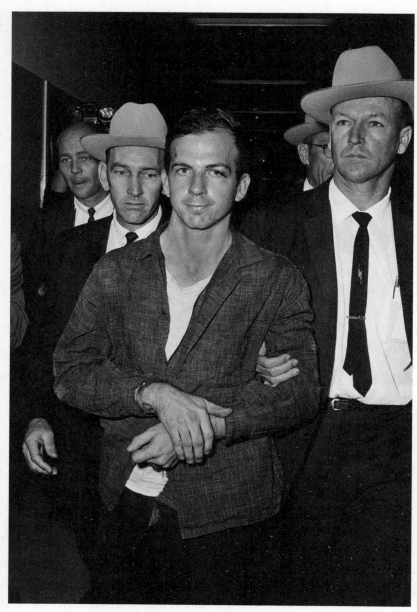

Lee Harvey Oswald: Alleged Assassin
PHOTO BY BILL WINFREY, COURTESY OF THE *DALLAS MORNING NEWS*

were and what they were doing when they heard the shocking news that President Kennedy had been shot and, shortly thereafter, that he had died. They have images of the charismatic young president and his wife arriving in Texas on Thursday, November 21, first visiting San Antonio to dedicate the United States Air Force School of Aerospace Medicine and Houston to attend a testimonial dinner. Then the Kennedys flew to Fort Worth to spend the night, and, on the morning of Friday, November 22, the president addressed the Chamber of Commerce there before flying to nearby Dallas.

Since it was a lovely fall day with temperatures in the high sixties, Kennedy said he did not want to use the protective bubble on the presidential limousine that would take him from the airport through the streets of Dallas to the Trade Mart where he was to address a luncheon gathering of Dallas business and civic leaders. He seated himself in the rear seat on the right. Texas Governor John Connally sat in a jump seat in front of him. Their wives sat to their left. Two Secret Service agents sat in the front seat.

Leading the motorcade were two cars containing Dallas Police Chief Jesse Curry and other members of the police force and Secret Service. Then came the presidential limousine, followed by a car with White House staff and more Secret Service agents, and a fifth car—another limousine—with Vice President Lyndon Johnson, his wife, and Texas Senator Ralph Yarborough. The remaining vehicles, a long line of them, held members of Congress, other dignitaries, photographers, more members of the White House staff, and others.

The motorcade left the Love Field airport about 11:50 a.m. As it made its way to and through downtown, crowds lined the streets—sometimes covering the sidewalks from the curb to the walls of buildings. Generally, the reception seemed to be friendly and enthusiastic. Just as the limousine turned into Dealey Plaza and headed north on Houston Street toward the Texas School Book Depository about a block ahead, Nellie Connally, the governor's wife, said to Kennedy, "Mr. President, you can't say Dallas doesn't love you."

The limousine made a fairly sharp curving turn left just in front of the book depository building to head west down the Elm Street hill leading beneath a railroad overpass. The president was still waving to the crowds along the route. It was about 12:30 p.m. when the shots rang out. Mrs. Connally turned to see the president put his hands up to his neck and then slump in the seat. Meanwhile, her husband doubled over after being hit by a bullet in his back. "No, no, no, no," he said. "My God, they are going to kill us all." In the backseat, Jacqueline Kennedy said, "They have shot my husband. . . . They have killed my husband." Then there was silence as the limousine sped toward Parkland Memorial Hospital where President Kennedy was pronounced dead at 1 p.m. from wounds in the neck and head. Connally, wounded in the back, wrist, and thigh, would recover.

Meanwhile, the whereabouts of Lee Harvey Oswald can be tracked through eyewitness accounts from the time he left for work that morning. About 7:10 a.m. Oswald knocked on Wesley Frazier's door in Irving. Oswald sometimes rode to work with Frazier, who also worked at the Texas School Book Depository. Frazier remembered seeing a package in the backseat of the car. "What's that?" he asked. "Curtain rods," Oswald replied. The two men arrived at the book depository shortly before eight o'clock.

Other coworkers reported seeing Oswald in the book depository at 11:55 a.m., prior to the shootings, and at 12:31 p.m., just after the shootings. He left the building at 12:33 before law enforcement officials closed it. He boarded a city bus heading west on Elm Street just past 12:40, but the bus got bogged in the traffic. Oswald got off the bus, walked to the Greyhound bus station, and took a taxicab to his rooming house in the Oak Cliff section of Dallas, arriving just before 1 p.m. He stayed only a few minutes, during which time he grabbed a pistol. Some time between 1:11 and 1:16 p.m. a Dallas policeman, J. D. Tippit, in his patrol car, pulled up alongside a man answering a description given by an eyewitness at Dealey Plaza who saw a slender man take aim and fire a rifle from a sixth-floor corner window of the book depository building. The man, Oswald, was walking along East Tenth Street in Oak Cliff. Tippit talked to him through the car window, a witness said later, then got out of the car. Oswald pulled out a handgun and shot Tippit "a number of times" before running off. Oswald first ducked into the entrance alcove of a shoe store and then into the Texas Theater. The shoe store manager had observed Oswald "acting in a suspicious manner" outside the shoe store, saw him enter the theater, and followed to alert the ticket clerk. The ticket clerk called the police. About the same time, a man named Temple Bowley had discovered Tippit's body lying facedown in the middle of Tenth Street. Bowley climbed into the officer's car and used the police radio to report the shooting. When police officers arrived and converged on the theater, they arrested Oswald after a brief struggle and, by 2 p.m., had him in custody at the police department building. By the end of the night, he had been booked and arraigned for the murders of both Tippit and Kennedy. Over a period of two days, Dallas police interrogated him several times for over thirteen hours total. He repeatedly denied killing either Kennedy or Tippit.

On Sunday morning, November 24, Oswald was being led through the basement of Dallas Police Headquarters as he was being transferred from the city jail to the county jail. At 11:21 a.m. a Dallas nightclub owner named Jack Ruby stepped out of the assembled crowd and shot Oswald once in the abdomen. Oswald died at 1:07 p.m. in Parkland Memorial Hospital—the same hospital in which Kennedy had died two days earlier.

Five days later, on November 29, President Lyndon Johnson created the Warren Commission, officially known as the President's Commission on the Assassination of President Kennedy. It was chaired by Chief Justice Earl Warren. For the next ten months the seven members, their counsels, and staff would examine evidence, interview over five hundred witnesses, and publish an 888-page report. The commission's conclusion was that Oswald acted alone in assassinating Kennedy. Three other US government investigations followed in 1968, 1975, and 1978–79. They agreed with the

Warren Commission's conclusion that Oswald fired the fatal shots. The last official investigation, however, conducted by the House Select Committee on Assassinations, did entertain the possibility of a conspiracy—or at least a second shooter (who missed) firing from the so-called grassy knoll on Dealey Plaza. The committee, however, "was unable to identify the other gunman or the extent of the conspiracy."

According to Gary Cornwell, deputy chief council for the Select Committee, a reexamination of evidence and the application of more sophisticated diagnostic equipment fifteen years after the assassination suggest that "Oswald was *not* the only shooter." That finding is based on the testimony from several witnesses who reported hearing a shot fired and/or seeing a puff of smoke from the area of the grassy knoll just west of the book depository building. The Warren Commission, Cornwell says, "perhaps rejected such testimony because they found no physical corroboration for it." The Select Committee, however, did, he claims, develop scientific evidence to corroborate the testimony—mostly through photographic evidence and acoustical analysis of 1963 radio transmissions from a police motorcycle at the scene suggesting there were four shots fired, the third of which came from the grassy knoll. Subsequently these findings were questioned by the FBI and a panel assembled by the National Research Council. The latter group argued that the police tape contained "cross-talk" from a second channel and was therefore inconclusive. So, even in official circles, the conspiracy controversy goes on and on.

What none of the investigations dispute is that Oswald was the shooter firing from a sixth-floor window in the book depository. And if he did that, as Cornwell says, "whatever else he may or may not have been, he was not *simply* a patsy." The array of evidence indicates that 1) Oswald purchased the Mannlicher-Carcano rifle found on the sixth floor of the book depository after the assassination; 2) that he was subsequently in possession of that rifle as shown in photos of him taken by his wife; 3) that he was an employee of the Texas School Book Depository and was seen in the building shortly before and immediately after the assassination; 4) that boxes stacked near the sixth floor window to create an apparent "sniper's nest" bore his fingerprint and palm print; 5) that Oswald's Mannlicher-Carcano fired the fatal bullets; 6) that shots came from the general vicinity of the sixth-floor window where the rifle and three shell casings were found; 7) that Oswald fled the book depository building immediately after the assassination; 8) that he killed a police officer approximately forty-five minutes later; and 9) that he resisted arrest. The most damaging evidence, of course, was the rifle. Oswald denied owning it and said his head must have been superimposed on someone else's body in the incriminating photograph.

Oswald's mother, Marguerite, was the only one who gave much credence to the claim that the picture of Lee Harvey with his guns was fabricated. Marina, Oswald's wife, testified in 1964 that she took photographs in late March 1963 of Oswald wearing a pistol in a holster, holding the Mannlicher-Carcano rifle and two Marxist newspapers. She took the photographs at Oswald's request, she said, and with his camera. He sent one of the prints, dated April 5, 1963, to his friend George de Mohrenschildt. The inscription on the back said, in Russian, "Hunter of fascists—ha ha ha!" and included Oswald's signature. Photographic experts have analyzed the photos and determined they were not altered. If they were being circulated in April 1963, Oswald was in possession of the rifle over seven months prior to the assassination. According to Edward Jay Epstein, Marguerite was aware of the photographs and helped Marina destroy one print Oswald had signed and inscribed to his daughter June. Marina shredded the photo and set fire to it soon after Oswald was arrested; Marguerite flushed the remains down the toilet.

Oswald bought the rifle and a .38 Smith & Wesson Model 10 revolver by mail order in March 1963, using the name A. Hidell. When Oswald was arrested, police found on him a fake Selective Service card in the name of Alek James Hidell, and both the rifle and the pistol had been shipped at separate times to Oswald's

Dallas post office box, "as ordered by A. J. Hidell." Later, in June 1963, Oswald rented a post office box in New Orleans and gave A. J. Hidell as an alternate name.

On April 10, 1963, Oswald allegedly attempted to assassinate retired US Major General Edwin Walker, a right-wing political leader, by firing at him through a window as Walker sat at a desk in his home in Dallas. The bullet missed Walker and passed through a wall. When Oswald returned home after the shooting, he told Marina what he had done, but the Dallas police considered him a suspect only after the Kennedy assassination. Ballistics studies on the Walker bullet were inconclusive because it was too badly damaged, but neutron activation tests later showed that it was "extremely likely" that it was made by the same manufacturer and for the same make of rifle as the two bullets that later struck Kennedy.

Throughout all the investigations a fairly comprehensive profile of Oswald emerged. He was born in New Orleans on October 18, 1939, and placed in a Lutheran orphanage when he was three by his widowed mother. He stayed there, as did his two older brothers, for thirteen months. When his mother remarried, she took her boys out of the orphanage and brought them to Benbrook, Texas, near Fort Worth. Within a few years she divorced and moved with her three sons to Fort Worth. Reports are that even as a child Oswald was said to be "withdrawn and temperamental." As he got older, records show there were other concerns about his behavior.

By 1952 the two older boys had jobs, so only Lee moved with his mother to New York, where a half-brother, John Pic, was stationed in the US Coast Guard. Oswald allegedly threatened Pic's wife with a knife and struck his mother, and his unacceptable behavior in school got him sent to detention. He underwent psychiatric assessment following truancy charges in the Bronx section of New York City. The psychiatrist recommended continued treatment after describing Oswald's "vivid fantasy life, turning on topics of omnipotence and power, through which he tries to compensate for his present shortcomings and frustrations." The psychiatrist's diagnosis found a "personality pattern disturbance with schizoid features and passive-aggressive tendencies." Rather than seek treatment, however, Oswald's mother returned with him to New Orleans in January of 1954. He was in and out of tenth grade there and then back in Fort Worth during the next two years. He never received a high school diploma.

He was apparently a voracious reader who found his books "in the back dusty shelves of libraries." He read Karl Marx and told his friends he was a Marxist by the time he was fifteen. He joined the Young People's Socialist League and wrote in his diary, "I was looking for a key to my environment, and then I discovered socialist literature." A year after he quit school at age sixteen, he joined the US Marines and eventually qualified as an aviation electronics operator, a position requiring security clearance. He was assigned to Atsugi Air Base in Japan in 1957, a base for CIA U-2 spy planes flying over the Soviet Union. At Atsugi he was twice court-martialed: once for being in possession of an unregistered handgun, and, in March of 1958, for using "provoking words" and fighting with a sergeant. Before returning to his base in California, Oswald also served in Taiwan and the Philippines, where he was once again court-martialed for unnecessarily firing his rifle into the jungle while on nighttime sentry duty. His interest in left-wing politics continued as he became an outspoken supporter of Fidel Castro and his revolution in Cuba. Oswald also subscribed to the Communist newspaper *Daily Worker*.

Saying his mother needed care, he was granted a hardship discharge from the Marines in 1959. After spending only a couple of days with his mother in Fort Worth, Oswald subsequently traveled to France, England, and Finland and went from Helsinki to the Soviet Union. In Moscow he applied to become a Soviet citizen. The application was rejected, and Oswald cut his wrist in a failed attempt at suicide. After a week in the hospital, during which time the Soviets put him under psychiatric observation, he was nevertheless allowed to remain in the country. By now it was January of 1960. Given work as an assembler at a radio and television factory in Minsk, Oswald met Marina Nikolaevna Prusakova, a nineteen-year-old pharmacy worker. They married in April and had a baby daughter by the time Oswald, now seemingly disillusioned with life in the Soviet Union, applied to take his family and return to the United States. That he did in June of 1962.

First settling in Fort Worth, the Oswalds later lived in Dallas and then New Orleans. Oswald worked at a variety of jobs, but he either quit or was fired after only a few months. While in New Orleans, in May 1963, Oswald wrote to the Fair Play for Cuba Committee proposing to set up a FPCC branch office in New Orleans. No one joined, but he stayed active handing out leaflets on street corners and debating on the pro-Castro side of the Cuban issue. In early August he was arrested for disturbing the peace after fighting another man on the street, found guilty, fined $10, and briefly jailed.

Marina returned to Dallas in September of 1963 to have their second child, another daughter born October 20. Oswald went to the Cuban Embassy in Mexico City in late September and attempted to get permission to travel to Cuba. His application was turned down as was his request for a visa for the Soviet Union. Back in Dallas by October 3, Oswald rented a room in Oak Cliff and left his wife and daughter in the home of a woman named Ruth Paine in Irving. It was Paine who helped him find a job at the Texas School Book Depository. He would visit his family on weekends and drive into work in Dallas on Monday mornings with Paine's neighbor, Buell Wesley Frazier. Normally Oswald rode to Irving with Frazier on Friday after work, but he told Frazier on Thursday, November 21, that he would like to drive to Irving to pick up some curtain rods for a Dallas apartment. The next morning he loaded a long bulky package, which actually contained the rifle he had been storing in Paine's garage, and carried it into the book depository with him. The Warren Commission reports that

Shortly after the assassination, the Mannlicher-Carcano rifle belonging to Oswald was found partially hidden between some cartons on the sixth floor and the improvised paper bag in which Oswald brought the rifle to the Depository was found close by the window from which the shots were fired.

Three spent cartridge cases lay on the floor near the southeast corner window.

Although the Warren Commission concluded that it could not "ascribe to him [Oswald] any one motive or group of motives," it nevertheless listed a number of possible motivating factors, including "an overriding hostility to his environment" and a perpetual discontentment with the world around him. Additionally, Oswald did not appear "to have been able to establish meaningful relationships with other people." Well before the assassination he had "expressed his hatred for American society and acted in protest against it." His commitment to Marxism and communism factored in as well, in the opinion of the commission. On a more personal rather than political note, the commission concluded that Oswald perhaps "sought for himself a place in history—a role as the 'great man' who would be recognized as having been in advance of his times."

John Douglas and Mark Olshaker, in the *The Anatomy of Motive,* describe Oswald as "just another paranoid loser who went from job to job, group to group, cause to cause, looking for something to believe in, something to make him significant." They argue that "the significant evidence—behavioral and forensic—points to Lee Harvey Oswald as the lone assassin." For one thing, they say, "Oswald's not the kind of person you'd bring into a conspiracy, even as a dupe, because you couldn't trust him." He was "too unreliable, too unpredictable, too much of a flake." So, they conclude:

unfortunately for all of us, when he climbed to his perch on the sixth floor of the Texas School Book Depository and aimed his 6.5 millimeter, bolt-action, clip-fed, Italian-made Mannlicher-Carcano rifle at the motorcade turning the corner into Dealey Plaza and passing a short distance below, he caught up with, then overtook, history. A few days later, Jack Ruby, another paranoid loser who thought with one bold act that he could become a hero, took his own shot at immortality.

CHAPTER EIGHTEEN

Charles Whitman
Tower Sniper

Summers are hot in central Texas, and by late morning it was clear that August 1, 1966, was going to be a scorcher with high temperatures predicted to be near one hundred degrees. Nevertheless, twenty-five-year-old Charles Joseph Whitman had on two layers of clothes when he parked his car in a lot near the Tower at the University of Texas in Austin a little before 11:30 a.m. Over his jeans and short-sleeved shirt he had on blue nylon workman's coveralls.

He took from the backseat of his car a footlocker, painted military-style olive drab, loaded it and some other items onto a dolly, and made his way to a service elevator on the ground floor of the Tower. A woman employee, thinking possibly that he was working as a repairman or making a delivery, had to turn the elevator on for him. "Thank you, ma'am," he said. "You don't know how happy this makes me." He punched the button for the twenty-seventh floor. Once there he had to lug the dolly up stairs to the twenty-eighth floor.

An observation deck receptionist on that floor intercepted him and asked what his business was there. He hit her twice in the head, probably with the butt of one of two guns he'd removed from his gear and now held in his hands, and dragged her behind a couch just before a young couple came into the reception area from the Tower's observation deck. They greeted him, the young man thinking that the guns Whitman held might be for shooting pigeons. Whitman acknowledged their greeting, said, "Hi, how are you?" and watched them exit down the stairs to the elevator. Then he turned the receptionist's desk on its side and pushed it and a chair in front of the doorway as a barricade.

Charles Whitman: Tower Sniper
PRINTS AND PHOTOGRAPHS COLLECTION, THE DOLPH BRISCO CENTER FOR AMERICAN HISTORY,
THE UNIVERSITY OF TEXAS AT AUSTIN, DI 7363

Before he could make his way to the observation deck, a family of tourists arrived, and two young men pushed the desk aside enough for one of them to begin squeezing by to see what was going on. Whitman shot him and his brother with a twelve-gauge sawed-off shotgun and fired on the rest of the family as they tumbled backward down the stairs. One of the young men and his aunt were killed by the blasts; his brother and mother were badly wounded.

Still in the reception area, Whitman placed the shotgun back in the footlocker, tied a white sweatband around his head, draped binoculars around his neck, and gathered up a knapsack filled with ammunition. He loaded the footlocker back on the dolly and wheeled it out onto the open-air deck and into the Austin heat. After unloading the dolly, he wedged it against the only door to the deck on the south side of the Tower. From below one of the huge gilded clocks on the 307-feet-tall structure, he looked south onto a large grassy mall stretching to Littlefield Fountain at the opposite edge of the UT campus. Beyond that was a view of the state capitol's dome. Students were beginning to empty out of the buildings on either side of the mall after their eleven-o'clock classes. Whitman leaned over the four-foot wall surrounding the deck, raised his rifle, sighted in through a powerful scope, and fired his first shot from the Tower at 11:48 a.m.

An eighteen-year-old female student, eight months pregnant, fell, shot through her stomach, colon, and uterus. The baby she carried died instantly. Whitman turned his sights on her boyfriend, also eighteen, as the young man knelt and reached out to his wounded girlfriend. Shot in the chest, he fell dead on top of her, pinning her on the searingly hot concrete on which she had fallen. Whitman then targeted a visiting physics professor and a Peace Corps trainee—both killed. His bullets hit two more students—both wounded and unmoving, playing dead. Moving to the west wall, he fired on and wounded two young women headed for lunch on the Drag, a popular shopping area across Guadalupe Street from the campus.

Within the first fifteen to twenty minutes Whitman had picked off most of his victims, randomly selecting targets within a five-block area: a young police officer, one of the first on the scene; an electrician walking toward his truck parked five hundred yards from the Tower; an Austin lifeguard and a young woman strolling along the Drag; a political scientist in town to do some research, browsing at a newsstand on Guadalupe Street; a university senior dropped and bleeding to death on the pavement. Would-be rescuers were forced to take cover and leave wounded victims lying in the open enduring the pain of their wounds and the skin-blistering heat of pavement and cement and fearing that they might be shot again.

When city policemen, highway patrolmen, Texas Rangers, and a contingent of US Secret Service men from President Lyndon Johnson's Austin office arrived on campus, Whitman ducked below the parapet and fired through the narrow rainspouts built into the wall around the deck. Civilians with hunting rifles joined the law enforcement respondents and began returning fire. A police sharpshooter went up in a small plane flown by the manager of a local flying school. The intense heat waves from the ground made it difficult for the pilot to hold the plane steady as it circled the Tower, and, of course, Whitman began shooting at the aircraft. As ineffective as it was as a way of getting at Whitman, the plane did draw Whitman's attention and fire away from those on the ground. And it allowed four men—three policemen and a deputized civilian—the opportunity to enter the Tower, make their way to the top floor, and step out onto the observation deck.

Houston McCoy, in his patrol car, was the first officer assigned the call at 11:53 a.m. to investigate a shooting near the UT Tower. He and another Austin Police Department officer, Larry Day, joined off-duty officer Ramiro (Ray) Martinez and a hastily deputized bookstore manager named Allen Crum on the twenty-eighth floor. Martinez recalls that he and Crum were the first out onto the observation deck after Martinez pushed against the glass door partially barricaded by the dolly wedged against it. The dolly fell over backward, making a clanging sound. If Whitman heard it, he didn't choose to investigate. Instead, he sat in the northwest corner of the Tower, his back against the north wall, his carbine in his hands.

Martinez opened the door "a little at a time," he said, and, see-ing no one, he and Crum stepped out on the deck. Martinez had his service pistol; Crum carried a rifle.

Crum aimed his rifle at the southwest corner; Martinez crawled toward the southeast corner, aware of friendly fire hitting all around him, and cautiously peered around the clock tower wall to the north-east. He couldn't see for the clock jutting out on the east side. Mean-while, Day had moved in behind Crum, and McCoy eased up behind Martinez. Crum accidentally discharged his weapon, and Whitman reacted by aiming his rifle back toward the southwest. Martinez stepped out in full view of Whitman and began firing his revolver before Whitman, now on his feet, could swing his rifle back and get off a shot. Almost simultaneously, McCoy hit Whitman twice in the head with blasts from his Winchester twelve-gauge shotgun. Mar-tinez said he then dropped his empty pistol and "grabbed the shot-gun from McCoy and fired," hitting the mortally wounded sniper in the upper left arm. It was now 1:42 p.m. Whitman's killing spree had lasted ninety-six minutes and left thirteen dead and thirty-one wounded on and around the campus. McCoy estimated it took "about a minute and a half" for him and the other three men to enter the observation deck and end the rampage.

A subsequent investigation would turn up two more bodies: Whitman's mother and his wife. He had killed them in the early hours of that Friday morning. He stabbed and shot his mother in her apartment and then returned home to bayonet his wife as she slept.

So just who was this Charles Whitman? His biography hardly seems one that would predict a mass murderer. He was born in 1941 into a wealthy, prominent family in Florida, was a gifted stu-dent, an accomplished pianist, a Roman Catholic altar boy, and an Eagle Scout—one of the youngest on record at age twelve. He rode his bicycle to make deliveries on his newspaper route. He was the pitcher on his parochial school's baseball team and manager of the football team. In short, he "had been an exemplary boy, the kind that neighborhood mothers hold up as a model to their own recalcitrant youngsters," as a *Time* magazine article pointed out just eleven days after the Tower shootings.

He grew into a handsome young man with clean-cut, All-American-boy blond good looks and enlisted in the US Marine Corps in July of 1959, just after he turned eighteen. He was a good Marine, judging from his awards: a Good Conduct Medal, the Marine Corps Expeditionary Medal, and a Sharpshooter's Badge. One of his Marine buddies, Larry Phillips, said Whitman "would do anything for members of his squad" and described a time Whitman managed to lift an overturned Jeep that had pinned Phillips underneath. "He was the kind of guy you would want around if you went into combat." Whitman never went into combat. Instead, he took the competitive examination for selection into the Naval Enlisted Science Education Program, a scholarship program designed to train engineers who would later become officers. He scored high on the examination, appeared before a selection committee, and was awarded a scholarship.

That is what brought him to Texas, where he was admitted to the University of Texas as a mechanical engineering student in September of 1961. While in Austin, he got involved in Scouting—where he taught the boys marksmanship—and he met and married Kathy Leissner from Needville, Texas. He sang in the Methodist church choir she attended in Austin.

In retrospect, however, there were indications that Whitman was a troubled individual and capable of violence. Reared by a demanding, authoritarian father who was "a fanatic about guns," Charlie and his two younger brothers were trained to use guns as soon as they were old enough to hold them. Like his father, Charlie admitted to having a temper and, like his father, to having beaten his wife "a few times." While he was in the Marine Corps, he was reprimanded for threatening to knock a fellow Marine's teeth out. It's likely that Whitman joined the Marines in the first place to escape his father, who once gave him a severe beating and threw him in the family swimming pool after Charlie came home drunk just before he turned eighteen.

Charlie had also gotten in trouble for breaking rules. While still living in a dormitory on the UT campus, he shot a deer and skinned it in his shower. As a result of that incident and low grades, his scholarship was withdrawn, and he was ordered back to active duty in North Carolina. There he was court-martialed for gambling, possessing an unauthorized personal firearm on base, and threatening another Marine over a gambling debt. He was sentenced to thirty days confinement and ninety days hard labor and was demoted from lance corporal to private. Nevertheless, he was honorably discharged from the Marines in December of 1964 and returned to the University of Texas, this time enrolling as an architectural engineering student.

He would sign up for as many as nineteen credit hours a semester and resort to the prescription drug Dexedrine as a stimulant to stay awake in class or for long study sessions. Complaining that the Dexedrine gave him terrible headaches, he also consumed large quantities of Excedrin. Friends and associates said he appeared to be very "uptight" and "really high strung." He perspired heavily and bit his fingernails. Then toward the end of the spring semester in 1966, Whitman's parents separated, and he drove to Florida to bring his mother back to Austin. His father began making persistent phone calls begging his wife to come back and asking Charlie to persuade her. Added to the pressures of school and the problems with drugs were these family concerns. He threatened to quit school and leave his wife. He did neither, but his mood swings prompted his wife to suggest that he visit the campus psychiatrist at the Student Health Center.

On March 29, 1966, roughly four months before the Tower shootings, Whitman saw Dr. Maurice Dean Heatly, the staff psychiatrist at the University Student Health Center. Heatly recalled that, on the one hand, Whitman "had something about him that suggested and expressed the all-American boy," but, on the other, that he "seemed to be oozing with hostility." During the session Whitman said he often thought "about going up on the Tower with a deer rifle and shooting people." In spite of these observations, Heatly concluded that Whitman was not a danger to himself or others but asked him to return at the same time the next week and urged him to call if he needed to talk. Whitman never returned and never called.

In a half-typed, half-handwritten note he left on his wife's body, he wrote, "Lately (I can't recall when it started) I have been a victim of many unusual and irrational thoughts." He mentioned talking with a doctor once for about two hours and trying to convey to him fears about having "overwhelming violent impulses." He continued, "After one session I never saw the doctor again, and since then I have been fighting my mental turmoil alone, and seemingly to no avail."

In the note Whitman also said, "After my death, I wish that an autopsy would be performed on me to see if there is any visible physical disorder. . . . Maybe research can prevent further tragedies of this type." Dr. Coleman de Chenar did perform an autopsy at the Cook Funeral Home the morning after the shootings. He noted that Whitman's skull was unusually thin and that he did have a small tumor in the middle part of his brain. Nevertheless, de Chenar did not believe the tumor had any correlation to psychosis or to Whitman's headaches.

Whitman's own writings reveal his intentions and his actions but do not clearly specify a motive. He began typing a letter dated Sunday, July 31, 1966, 6:45 p.m., by saying, "I don't quite understand what it is that compels me to type this letter. Perhaps it is to leave some vague reason for the actions I have recently performed." He hadn't yet performed his actions but no doubt anticipated someone's reading the letter after he and his victims were dead. Even he couldn't state a specific reason for the murders he would commit, as he indicated in this passage:

> It was after much thought that I decided to kill my wife, Kathy, tonight after I pick her up from work at the telephone company. I love her dearly, and she has been as fine a wife to me as any man could ever hope to have. I cannot rationaly [sic] pinpoint any specific reason for doing this. I don't know whether it is selfishness, or if I don't want her to have to face

the embarrassment my actions would surely cause her. At this time, though, the prominent reason in my mind is that I truly do not consider this world worth living in, and am prepared to die, and I do not want to leave her to suffer alone in it. I intend to kill her as painlessly as possible.

He would later stab her five times in the chest as she lay sleeping in their bed.

His first victim was his mother. He wrote a letter he left on her body as well. Handwritten on a yellow legal pad, it too was dated: Monday, 8-1-66, 12:30 a.m. It began, "I have just taken my mother's life. I am very upset over having done it." He then wrote that he had "relieved her of her suffering" at the hands of his father, presumably, for whom Whitman had an "intense hatred." The note concludes, "I am truly sorry that this is the only way I could see to relieve her sufferings but I think it was best. Let there be no doubt in your mind that I loved that woman with all my heart. If there exists a God let him understand my actions and judge me accordingly."

In the margin of the half-typed, half-handwritten note found by Kathy's body, Whitman added this notation: "8-1-66 Mon. 3:00 a.m. <u>Both Dead</u>." He wrote four more notes, one each to his two brothers and his father and one he left on the dresser beside two cameras. "Have the film developed in these cameras," he instructed. The photos showed nothing more than a livestock show and carnival held the previous March and other snapshots from trips to San Antonio and to Austin's Town Lake. The notes to his brothers were both dated 8-1-66 Monday 3:00 a.m. To his brother John, he said, "I am terribly sorry to have let you down. Please try to do better than I have. It won't be hard." The note to his brother Pat suggests the ongoing divisions within the family: "You are so wrong about Mom," Whitman wrote. "Maybe some day you will understand why she left Daddy."

In their book *The Anatomy of Motive,* John Douglas and Mark Olshaker speculate that Whitman's motive "was to make the statement about himself and the people around him he'd been trying to make unsuccessfully for many years." That "statement" evolves from what Douglas and Olshaker describe as the "assassin personality." According to their profile, these personalities tend to be "functional paranoiacs" but not paranoid schizophrenics. They "may be delusional, but they're not hallucinatory." Typically they are "male loners with self-esteem problems." The end result of their actions may be "a senseless act of mass killing rather than a targeted assassination of a political figure or celebrity."

Assassins are generally not leaders, say Douglas and Olshaker, and "most of them come from troubled childhoods." One way they compensate, oftentimes, is through "gun fetishism," seeing guns as means of empowerment. They often keep diaries or journals, as Whitman did. "In many cases, they actually use this journal writing to program themselves to commit the crime." Whatever the cause, "Charles Whitman chose to do what he did fully mindful of the consequences and moral implications," according to Douglas and Olshaker.

A commission appointed by Governor John Connally to probe into the question of why Whitman did what he did was made up of a distinguished panel of psychiatrists and scientists. They were unable to come up with an answer. "Without a recent psychiatric evaluation of Charles J. Whitman," they concluded, "the task force finds it impossible to make a formal psychiatric diagnosis."

What is known is that Whitman perpetrated one of the worst mass murders in modern United States history. At the time, it was the nation's worst. Gary Lavergne, author of a book about the shootings, says they "introduced us to the modern concept of what is now called simultaneous mass murder."

The Tower, "a symbol of a premier university and a very tragic event all at the same time," now has iron barriers to deter suicides, and observation deck tours are available by reservation only through the Texas Union Information Center. Tickets are six dollars per person, and tours are conducted only on weekends and on selected evenings during the summer. Just north of the main building is the Tower Garden, a grassy, tree-covered site dedicated August 1, 1999, "to the memory of all those who died and those whose lives were touched" by the tragedy thirty-three years before.

Bibliography

JEAN LAFITTE

Ackerly, Mary Gertrude. "Pirate Jean LaFitte Adds Mystery to La Porte History." *La Porte Liberal,* ca. 1949. Archived in La Porte Library vertical files.

Davis, William C. *Lone Star Rising: The Revolutionary Birth of the Texas Republic.* New York: Free Press, 2004.

Dobie, J. Frank. "Laffite and Pirate Booty." *Coronado's Children: Tales of Lost Mines and Buried Treasures of the Southwest.* Austin: University of Texas Press, [1930] 1978. 274–97.

"Jean Lafitte: Buccaneer of Barataria Bay." *Reader's Digest American Folklore and Legend.* Pleasantville, NY: Reader's Digest Assn., 1978. 80–81.

"The Legend of Jean Lafitte." Kemah Historical Society (www.kemahhistoricalsociety.net/legendl.html). Accessed June 1, 2009.

Lewis, Carroll A. Jr., *Treasures of Galveston Bay.* Quoted in La Porte Bay Area Heritage Society Newsletter. Eds. Fred and Pat Muston. July 2005.

Syers, Ed. "Napoleon's Place of Refuge." *Off the Beaten Trail.* Waco, TX: Texian, 1971. 226–30.

Warren, Harris Gaylord. "Lafitte, Jean." *The Handbook of Texas Online.* Texas State Historical Association (www.tshaonline .org/handbook/online/articles/LL/fla12.html). Accessed June 1, 2009.

Yoakum, Henderson K. *History of Texas from Its First Settlement in 1685 to Its Annexation to the United States in 1846.* Austin, TX: Steck, [1855] 1935.

JIM BOWIE

Baugh, Virgil E. *Rendezvous at the Alamo: Highlights in the Lives of Bowie, Crockett, and Travis.* New York: Pageant, 1960.

Davis, William C. *Three Roads to the Alamo: The Lives and Fortunes of Davy Crockett, Jim Bowie, and William Barrett Travis.* New York: Harper Collins, 1998.

Dobie, J. Frank. "The Legend of the San Saba or Bowie Mine." *Legends of Texas.* Ed. J. Frank Dobie. Publications of the Texas Folklore Society No. III. Reprint ed. Hatboro, PA: Folklore Associates, [1924] 1964. 12–20.

————. "The Lost San Saba Mine." *Coronado's Children: Tales of Lost Mines and Buried Treasures of the Southwest.* Austin: University of Texas Press, [1930] 1978. 3–52.

Eckhardt, C. F. *The Lost San Saba Mines.* Austin: Texas Monthly Press, 1982.

Flynn, Jean. *Jim Bowie: A Texas Legend.* Burnet, TX: Eakin, 1980.

Weddle, Robert S. *The San Saba Mission: Spanish Pivot in Texas.* Austin: University of Texas Press, 1964.

Wilbarger, J. W. "Bowie's Victory." *Indian Depredations in Texas.* Austin, TX: Hutchings, 1889. 91–98.

Williamson, William R. "Bowie, James." *The Handbook of Texas Online.* Texas State Historical Association (www.tshaonline .org/handbook/online/articles/fbo45). Accessed Feb. 17, 2011.

PAMELIA MANN

Davis, Joe Tom. "Pamelia Mann: She Did It Her Way." *Legendary Texians.* Vol. 2. Austin, TX: Eakin, 1985. 27–40.

Davis, William C. *Lone Star Rising: The Revolutionary Birth of the Texas Republic.* New York: Free Press, 2004.

Dobie, J. Frank. "How Texas was Hell on Women." *The Flavor of Texas.* Austin, TX: Jenkins, 1975. 51–58.

Haley, James L. *Texas: An Album of History.* Garden City, NY: Doubleday, 1985.

Hardin, Stephen L. *Texian Iliad: A Military History of the Texas Revolution, 1835–1836.* Austin: University of Texas Press, 1994.

Hogan, William Ransom. "Pamelia Mann: Texas Frontierswoman." *Southwest Review,* vol. 20 (1935). 360–70.

Kearby, Mike. Mike Kearby's Texas: October 2008 (http://mikekearbystexas.blogspot.com/2008_10_01_archive.html). Accessed May 3, 2011.

McDonald, Archie P. "Pamelia Mann: Tough Texan." (www.texasescapes.com/AllThingsHistorical/Pamelia-Mann-Tough-Texan-AM1107.html). Accessed May 3, 2011.

Moore, Karen. "Mann, Pamelia Dickinson." *The Handbook of Texas Online.* Texas State Historical Association (www.tshaonline.org/handbook/online/articles/fma35). Accessed May 3, 2011.

Moore, Stephen L. *Eighteen Minutes: The Battle of San Jacinto and the Texas Independence Campaign.* Dallas: Republic of Texas, 2004.

Smithwick, Noah. *The Evolution of a State or Recollections of Old Texas Days.* Austin: University of Texas Press, [1900] 1983.

Yoakum, Henderson K. *History of Texas from Its First Settlement in 1685 to Its Annexation to the United States in 1846.* Austin, TX: Steck, [1855] 1935.

Mirabeau B. Lamar

De Shields, James T. *Border Wars of Texas.* Waco, TX: Texian, 1976.

Fehrenbach, T. R. *Lone Star: A History of Texas and the Texans.* New York: Macmillan, 1968.

Marks, Paula Mitchell. *Turn Your Eyes Toward Texas: Pioneers Sam and Mary Maverick.* College Station: Texas A&M UP, 1989.

Maverick, Mary A. *Memoirs of Mary A. Maverick.* Lincoln, NE: University of Nebraska Press, [1921] 1989.

Mayhall, Mildred P. *Indian Wars of Texas.* Waco, TX: Texian, 1965.

McCraw, William. "Mirabeau B. Lamar." *Professional Politicians.* Washington, DC: Imperial Press, 1940. 53–88.

McLeod, Hugh. "McLeod's Report of the Council House Fight, March 20, 1840." *Indian Relations in Texas.* Texas State Library & Archives Commission (www.tsl.state.tx.us/exhibits/indian/war/mcleod-mar1840-l.html). Accessed March 6, 2011.

Nichols, James Wilson. "The Council House Fight and Battle of Plum Creek." *The Journal of James Wilson Nichols 1820–1887.* Sons of Dewitt Colony Texas (www.tamu.edu/faculty/ccbn/dewitt/plumcreeknichols.htm). Accessed March 6, 2011.

Roland, Charles P. *Albert Sidney Johnston: Soldier of Three Republics.* Austin: University of Texas Press, 1964.

Schitz, Jodye Lynn Dickson. "Council House Fight." *The Handbook of Texas Online.* Texas State Historical Association (www.tshaonline.org/handbook/online/articles/btc01). Accessed March 6, 2011.

Siegel, Stanley. *The Poet President of Texas: The Life of Mirabeau B. Lamar, President of the Republic of Texas.* Austin, TX: Jenkins, 1977.

Smithwick, Noah. *The Evolution of a State or Recollections of Old Texas Days.* Austin: University of Texas Press, [1900] 1983.

Wallace, Ernest, and E. Adamson Hoebel. *The Comanches: Lords of the South Plains.* Norman: University of Oklahoma Press, 1952.

Webb, Walter Prescott. *The Texas Rangers: A Century of Frontier Defense.* Austin: University of Texas Press, [1935] 1993.

Judge Roy Bean

Davis, Joe Tom. "Roy Bean: Barroom Judge and Con Man." *Legendary Texians*. Vol. 2. Austin, TX: Eakin, 1985. 155–74.

Eckhardt, C. F. "The Man Who Became Judge Roy Bean." *Tales of Badmen, Bad Women, and Bad Places: Four Centuries of Texas Outlawry*. Lubbock: Texas Tech UP, 1999. 39–51.

Erdoes, Richard. "An' That's My Roolin'." *Legends and Tales of the American West*. New York: Pantheon, 1991.

Estleman, Loren D. *Roy & Lillie: A Love Story*. New York: Tom Doherty, 2010.

McDaniel, Ruel. *Vinegaroon: The Saga of Judge Roy Bean, "Law West of the Pecos."* Kingsport, TN: Southern, 1936.

Sonnichsen, C. L. "Bean, Roy." *The Handbook of Texas Online*. Texas State Historical Association (www.tshaonline.org/handbook/online/articles/fbe08). Accessed October 6, 2010.

———. *Roy Bean: Law West of the Pecos*. Old Greenwich, CT: Devin-Adair, 1943.

Sterling, William Warren. *Trials and Trails of a Texas Ranger*. Norman: University of Oklahoma Press, 1968.

Leander McNelly

"Captain Leander McNelly Special Force." Frontier Battalion Texas Rangers Exhibit: Texas Ranger Memorial (www.fbtre.org/texas-ranger-memorial). Accessed April 27, 2011.

Cutrer, Thomas W. "McNelly, Leander H." *The Handbook of Texas Online*. Texas State Historical Association (www.tshaonline.org/handbook/online/articles/fmcag). Accessed April 27, 2011.

Davis, Joe Tom. "L. H. McNelly: The Ranger Who Kept on Coming." *Legendary Texians*. Vol. 2. Austin, TX: Eakin, 1985. 103–25.

Durham, George. *Taming the Nueces Strip: The Story of McNelly's Rangers*. Austin: University of Texas Press, 1962.

Jennings, N. A. *A Texas Ranger*. New York: Scribner's. 1899.

"Leander Harvey McNelly 1844–1877." Texas Ranger Hall of Fame and Museum (www.texasranger.org/halloffame/McNelly_ Leander.htm). Accessed April 27, 2011.

"Leander H. McNelly Papers." San Jacinto Museum of History (www.sanjacinto-museum.org/Herzstein_Library/Manuscripts/ Finding_Aids/McNelly). Accessed April 27, 2011.

Utley, Robert M. *Lone Star Justice: The First Century of the Texas Rangers*. New York: Oxford University Press, 2002.

Webb, Walter Prescott. *The Texas Rangers: A Century of Frontier Defense*. Austin: University of Texas Press, [1935] 1985.

BELLE STARR

Anderson, John Q. "Belle Starr and the Biscuit Dough." *Singers and Storytellers*. Eds. Mody C. Boatright, Wilson M. Hudson, and Allen Maxwell. Dallas, TX: Southern Methodist University Press, 1961. 156–65.

Arnott, Richard. "Belle Starr." *Wild West* (www.historynet.com/ belle-starr.htm.) Accessed September 6, 2010.

Green, Carl R., and William R. Sanford. *Belle Starr*. Hillside, NJ: Enslow, 1992.

Metz, Leon C. "Starr, Myra Maybelle Shirley." *The Handbook of Texas Online*. Texas State Historical Association (www.tsha-online.org/handbook/online/articles/SS/fstbl.html). Accessed September 6, 2010.

Naden, Corinne J., and Rose Blue. *Belle Starr and the Wild West*. Woodbridge, CT: Blackbirch, 2000.

Rau, Margaret. *Belle of the West: The True Story of Belle Starr.* Greensboro, NC: Morgan Reynolds, 2001.

Shirley, Glenn. *Belle Starr and Her Times: The Literature, the Facts, the Legends.* Norman: University of Oklahoma Press, 1982.

Winegarten, Ruth. "Belle Starr: The Bandit Queen of Dallas." *Legendary Ladies of Texas.* Ed. Francis Edward Abernathy. Dallas: University of North Texas Press, 1994. 39–49.

Young, Richard, and Judy Dockrey Young. "Belle and the Stuff of Legends." *Outlaw Tales: Legends, Myths, and Folklore from America's Middle Border.* Little Rock, AR: August House, 1992. 21–44.

SAM BASS

"The Ballad of Sam Bass." *Cowboy Songs and Other Frontier Ballads.* Collected by John A. Lomax. New York: Sturgis, 1910.

Dobie, J. Frank. "Sam Bass, Texas Robin Hood." *The Life Treasury of American Folklore.* New York: Time, 1961. 192–95.

Eckhardt, C. F. "The Ballad of Sam Bass." *Tales of Bad Men, Bad Women, and Bad Places: Four Centuries of Texas Outlawry.* Lubbock: Texas Tech University Press, 1999. 87–109.

Gillett, James B. *Six Years with the Texas Rangers, 1875–1881.* New Haven, CT: Yale University Press, 1925.

Matthews, Jim. "Shootout in Texas." *Accent West.* July 2004. 45–47.

Syers, William Edward. "Short Sad Life of Sam Bass." *Off the Beaten Track.* Waco, TX: Texian, 1971. 184–87.

Utley, Robert M. *Lone Star Justice: The First Century of the Texas Rangers.* New York: Oxford University Press, 2002.

Webb, Walter Prescott. "Sam Bass: Texas's Beloved Bandit." *The Texas Rangers: A Century of Frontier Defense.* Austin: University of Texas Press, [1935] 1985. 371–91.

JOHN WESLEY HARDIN

Davis, Joe Tom. *Legendary Texians*. Vol. 2. Austin, TX: Eakin, 1985.

Douglas, C. L. *Famous Texas Feuds*. Austin, TX: State House, [1936] 1988.

Eckhardt, C .F. "The Ballad of Sam Bass." *Tales of Bad Men, Bad Women, and Bad Places: Four Centuries of Texas Outlawry*. Lubbock: Texas Tech University Press, 1999. 87–109.

Hardin, John Wesley. *The Life of John Wesley Hardin As Written by Himself*. Norman: University of Oklahoma Press, [1896] 1961.

Metz, Leon C. "Hardin, John Wesley." *The Handbook of Texas Online*. Texas State Historical Association (www.tshaonline.org/handbook/online/articles/fha63). Accessed March 24, 2011.

Smallwood, James. M. *The Feud That Wasn't: The Taylor Ring, Bill Sutton, John Wesley Hardin, and Violence in Texas*. College Station: Texas A&M UP, 2008.

Sonnichsen, C. L. "The Grave of John Wesley Hardin." *The Grave of John Wesley Hardin: Three Essays on Grassroots History*. College Station: Texas A&M Press, 1979. 57–90.

Trachtman, Paul. "Sinister Masters of Murder." *The Gunfighters*. Chicago: Time-Life, 1974. 166–93.

O. HENRY

"The Caballero's Way." *Collected Stories of O. Henry*. New York: Avenel, 1986. 853–60.

Caravantes, Peggy. *Writing Is My Business: The Story of O. Henry*. Greensboro, NC: Morgan Reynolds, 2006.

Glassman, Peter. "Afterword." *The Gift of the Magi and Other Stories*. O. Henry. New York: William Morrow, 1997. 203–5.

Henry, O. "Blind Man's Holiday." *Collected Stories of O. Henry*. New York: Avenel, 1986. 738–49.

———. "A Call Loan." *Collected Stories of O. Henry.* New York: Avenel, 1986. 292–94.

———. "A Departmental Case." *Collected Stories of O. Henry.* New York: Avenel, 1986. 187–94.

———. "Friends in San Rosario." *Collected Stories of O. Henry.* New York: Avenel, 1986. 140–47.

———. "The Guardian of the Scutcheon." *Collected Stories of O. Henry.* New York: Avenel, 1986. 194–98.

———. "Hygeia at the Solito." *Collected Stories of O. Henry.* New York: Avenel, 1986. 215–22.

———. "The Roads We Take." *Collected Stories of O. Henry.* New York: Avenel, 1986. 523–26.

Horowitz, Paul J. "Foreword." *Collected Stories of O. Henry.* New York: Avenel, 1986. x–xii.

———. "Introduction." *Collected Stories of O. Henry.* New York: Avenel, 1986. xiii–xvii.

O'Quinn, Trueman E. and Jenny Lind Porter. *Time to Write: How William Sidney Porter Became O. Henry.* Austin, TX: Eakin, 1986.

Patterson, Connie. "Porter, William Sydney." *The Handbook of Texas Online.* Texas State Historical Association (www.tshaonline .org/handbook/online/articles/fpo20). Accessed January 8, 2011.

"William Sydney Porter (O. Henry)." *A Treasury of American Literature.* Vol. 2. Eds. Joe Lee Davis, John T. Frederick, and Frank Luther Mott. New York: Grolier, 1955. 396–97.

GREGORIO CORTEZ

Convis, Charles L. "Border Bandits." *Outlaw Tales of Texas.* Guilford, CT: Twodot, 2008. 97–107.

Dobie, J. Frank. *The Mustangs.* New York: Little, Brown, 1934.

Paredes, Américo. *With His Pistol in His Hand: A Border Ballad and Its Hero.* Austin: University of Texas Press, 1958.

Rodriguez, Juan Carlos. "El Corrido de Gregorio Cortez." *The Handbook of Texas Online.* Texas State Historical Association (www .tshaonline.org/handbook/online/articles/xee02). Accessed May 8, 2011.

Sterling, William Warren. "Gregorio Cortez." *Trails and Trials of a Texas Ranger.* Norman: University of Oklahoma Press, 1959. 496–516.

Utley, Robert M. *Lone Star Justice: The First Century of the Texas Rangers.* New York: Oxford University Press, 2002.

MIRIAM AMANDA "MA" FERGUSON

Alter, Judy. *Miriam "Ma" Ferguson: First Woman Governor of Texas.* Abilene, TX: State House Press, 2006.

Brown, Norman D. *Hood, Bonnet, and Little Brown Jug: Texas Politics, 1921–1928.* College Station: Texas A&M University Press, 1984.

Huddleston, John D. "Ferguson, Miriam Amanda Wallace." *The Handbook of Texas Online.* Texas State Historical Association (www.tsha.utexas.edu/handbook/online/articles/FF/ffe6.html) Accessed October 26, 2010.

———. "Highway Development: A 'Concrete' History of Twentieth-Century Texas." *Texas: A Sesquicentennial Celebration.* Ed. Donald W. Whisenhunt. Austin, TX: Eakin, 1984. 253–67.

Jones, Billy M. "Miriam Amanda Ferguson." *Women of Texas.* Waco, TX: Texian, 1972. 157–73.

Maxwell, Robert S. "Texas in the Progressive Era, 1900–1930." *Texas: A Sesquicentennial Celebration.* Ed. Donald W. Whisenhunt. Austin, TX: Eakin, 1984. 173–200.

Paulissen, Maisie. "Pardon Me, Governor Ferguson." *Legendary Ladies of Texas*. Ed. Francis Edward Abernathy. Denton: University of North Texas Press, 1994. 145–61.

Paulissen, May Nelson, and Carl Randall McQueary. *Miriam: The Southern Belle Who Became the First Woman Governor of Texas*. Austin, TX: Eakin, 1995.

Richardson, Rupert N., Adrian Anderson, and Ernest Wallace. *Texas: The Lone Star State*. Englewood Cliffs, NJ: Prentice Hall, 1993.

Whisenhunt, Donald W. "Contemporary Texas." *Texas: A Sesquicentennial Celebration*. Ed. Donald W. Whisenhunt. Austin, TX: Eakin, 1984. 201–23.

H. L. HUNT

Burrough, Bryan. *The Big Rich: The Rise and Fall of the Greatest Oil Fortunes*. New York: Penguin, 2009.

Burst, Ardis. *The Three Families of H. L. Hunt*. New York: Weidenfeld & Nicolsson, 1988.

Hurt, Harry III. *Texas Rich: The Hunt Dynasty from the Early Oil Days through the Silver Crash*. New York: Norton, 1981.

Palmer, Jerrell Dean. "Hunt, Haroldson Lafayette." *The Handbook of Texas Online*. Texas State Historical Association (www.tsha online.org/handbook/online/articles/fhu59). Accessed November 10, 2010.

Presley, James. *Saga of Wealth: The Rise of the Texas Oilmen*. Austin: Texas Monthly, 1983.

GEORGE B. PARR

Anders, Evan. *Boss Rule in South Texas: The Progressive Era*. Austin: University of Texas Press, 1979.

Anders, Evan. "George Berham Parr." *The Handbook of Texas Online.* Texas State Historical Association (www.tshaon-line.org/handbook/online/articles/PP/fpa36.html). Accessed August 25, 2010.

Caro, Robert A. *Means of Ascent (The Years of Lyndon Johnson).* New York: Knopf, 1990.

Clark, John E. *The Fall of the Duke of Duval: A Prosecutor's Journal.* Austin, TX: Eakin, 1995.

Dallek, Robert. *Lone Star Rising: Lyndon Johnson and His Times 1908–1960.* New York: Oxford University Press, 1991.

"Death of a Duke." *Time,* April 14, 1975 (www.time.com/time/magazine/article/0,9171,917281,00.html). Accessed August 25, 2010.

"The Duke Delivers." *Time,* September 27, 1948 (www.time.com/time/magazine/article/0,9171,780017,00.html). Accessed August 25, 2010.

Lynch, Dudley. *The Duke of Duval: The Life and Times of George B. Parr.* Waco, TX: Texian, 1976.

BONNIE PARKER

Barrow, Blanche Caldwell. *My Life with Bonnie and Clyde.* Norman: University of Oklahoma Press, 2004.

Eckhardt, C. F. "The Real Story of Bonnie and Clyde." *Tales of Bad Men, Bad Women, and Bad Places: Four Centuries of Texas Outlawry.* Lubbock: Texas Tech UP, 1999. 178–203.

Frost, H. Gordon, and John H. Jenkins. *"I'm Frank Hamer": The Life of a Texas Peace Officer.* Austin, TX: Pemberton, 1968.

Guinn, Jeff. *Go Down Together: The True, Untold Story of Bonnie and Clyde.* New York: Simon & Schuster, 2009.

Hinton, Ted. *Ambush: The Real Story of Bonnie and Clyde.* Brian, TX: Shoal Creek, 1979.

Maddox, Web. "Clyde Barrow and Bonnie Parker." *The Black Sheep.* Quanah, TX: Nortex, 1975. 5–46.

Phillips, John Neal. *Running with Bonnie and Clyde: The Ten Fast Years of Ralph Fults.* Norman: University of Oklahoma Press, 1996.

———, and Andre L. Gorzell. "'Tell Them I Don't Smoke Cigars': The Story of Bonnie Parker." *Legendary Ladies of Texas.* Publications of the Texas Folklore Society Number XLIII. Ed. Francis Edward Abernathy. Denton: University of North Texas Press, 1994.

Webb, Walter Prescott. *The Texas Rangers: A Century of Frontier Defense.* Austin: University of Texas Press, [1935] 1993.

MADALYN MURRAY O'HAIR

Dracos, Ted. *Ungodly: The Passions, Torments, and Murder of Atheist Madalyn Murray O'Hair.* New York: Free Press, 2003.

Lancaster, Katherine. "O'Hair, Madalyn Murray." *The Handbook of Texas Online.* Texas State Historical Association (www.tsha online.org/handbook/online/articles/foh23). Accessed January 31, 2011.

Milloy, Ross E. "Bodies Identified as Those of Missing Atheist and Kin." *The New York Times,* March 16, 2001 (www.nytimes .com/2001/03/16/bodies-identified-as-those-of-missing-atheist-and-kin.html?ref=madalynmurrayohair). Accessed February 8, 2011.

Seaman, Ann Rowe. *America's Most Hated Woman: The Life and Gruesome Death of Madalyn Murray O'Hair.* New York: Continuum, 2005.

LEE HARVEY OSWALD

Cornwell, Gary. *Real Answers.* Spicewood, TX: Paleface, 1998.

Douglas, John, and Mark Olshaker. *The Anatomy of Motive.* New York: Scribner, 1999.

Epstein, Edward Jay. *Legend: The Secret World of Lee Harvey Oswald.* New York: McGraw-Hill, 1978.

Garrison, Jim. *On the Trail of the Assassins.* New York: Sheridan Square, 1988.

Hurt, Henry. *Reasonable Doubt: An Investigation into the Assassination of John F. Kennedy.* New York: Holt, Rinehart and Winston, 1985.

Lifton, David S. *Best Evidence: Disguise and Deception in the Assassination of John F. Kennedy.* New York: Macmillan, 1980.

Mailer, Norman. *Oswald's Tale: An American Mystery.* New York: Random House, 1995.

Minutaglio, Bill. "Lee Harvey Oswald: A Life without an Anchor." *November 22: The Day Remembered.* Dallas, TX: Taylor, 1990. 120–26.

Northcott, Kaye. "The Last Days of Lee Harvey Oswald." *Texas Co-op Power.* November 2005. 16–18.

Report of the President's Commission on the Assassination of President Kennedy. Washington: GPO, 1964.

Stafford, Jean. *A Mother in History.* New York: Farrar, Straus and Giroux, 1966.

Summers, Anthony. *Conspiracy.* New York: McGraw-Hill, 1980.

CHARLES WHITMAN

Barr, Alwyn. "Whitman, Charles Joseph." *The Handbook of Texas Online.* Texas State Historical Association (www.tshaonline.org/handbook/online/articles/fwh42). Accessed November 23, 2010.

Colloff, Pamela. "96 Minutes." *Texas Monthly.* August 2006. 102–9.

Douglas, John, and Mark Olshaker. *The Anatomy of Motive.* New York: Scribner, 1999.

Gándara, Ricardo. "Beyond Tower Sniper's Sights." *Austin American-Statesman,* May 14, 2011. A1, A11.

Lavergne, Gary M. *A Sniper in the Tower: The Charles Whitman Murders.* Denton: University of North Texas Press, 1997.

Martinez, Ramiro. "The University of Texas Tower Sniper." *They Call Me Ranger Ray.* New Braunfels, TX: Rio Bravo, 2005.

"The Tower." *Mass Murderers.* True Crime Series. Alexandria, VA: Time-Life Books, 1992. 31–56.

INDEX

A

Abilene, TX, 93
Abington School District v. Schempp, 161
Abramovitz, Susan, 161, 163
Alamo, 11, 16, 19–20, 21
Alexander, Andrew J., 60–61
American Atheist Forum, 166
American Atheists, 164–65, 167
Anatomy of Motive (Douglas), 181–82, 191–92
Anson, TX, 117
Apaches, 16–17
assassination, 171–82, 192
astronauts, 165
atheism, 164–65
Aury, Louis Michael, 2
Austin, Stephen F., 15, 18–19
Austin, TX, 37, 98, 99, 127, 164, 183–92

B

Bandit Queen, 62–71
Barrow, Buck and Blanche, 153–55, 155
Barrow, Clyde, 151–60. *See also* Parker, Bonnie
    captured and killed, 157
    films about, 160
    loyalty of Bonnie Parker, 158
    as murderer, 153
    prison escape, 156–57
Bass, Sam, 72–84
    death of, 82
    double crossed by Jim Murphy, 79–81
    as gang leader, 78
    generosity, 83–84
    hunted and captured by Texas Rangers, 78–79, 81–82
    money management skills, 74–75
    as robber, 75–78
Bean, Roy, 41–50
    brushes with the law, 47–48
    death of, 50
    early life, 41
    as fight promoter, 48–49
    as judge, 45–47
    as justice of the peace, 44, 48
    methods of conducting inquests, 46
    as murderer, 47
    as saloon owner, 43–44
    as thief, 43
Bexar. *See* San Antonio, TX
bigamy, 134
Bonham, James, 11
Bonnie and Clyde. *See* Barrow, Clyde; Parker, Bonnie
bossism, 150
Bowen, Jane, 93–94
Bowie, Jim, 11–20
    and the Alamo battle, 19–20
    allegiance to Mexico, 15
    arrested, 18

death of, 20
early life, 13
involvement in politics, 18
and land speculation, 14, 18
legends about, 16
marriage, 16
as murderer, 14–15
as robber, 17–18
and silver mining, 16–17
as slave trader, 13–14
in volunteer militia, 18–19
Bowie, Rezin, 13, 17
Bowles, Chief, 35
Box Thirteen, 145, 146, 148, 150
Boyd, Percy, 159–60
brothel owner, 21–30
Buffalo Hump, Chief, 36, 37
Bunker, Lyda, 134, 138–39
Burnet, David G., 22

C

Campeche, 3
cattle rustlers, 59–61
Champs d'Aisle, 9–10
Cherokees, 34, 35
Chisholm Trail, 92
Civil War, 51–52, 70
Claiborne, William C. C., 1
Coahuila, 18
Coleman, Robert, 22
Comanches, 31–34, 35–37, 40
Communist Party, 164
Connally, John, 149, 173, 174, 192
Conner, T. E. "Ted," 43
Cornwell, Gary, 176
corsairs, 1, 2

Cortez, Gregorio, 107–18
arrested, 115
death of, 117
eludes police for 10 days, 115–16
held in jail, 116
hunted as killer of two sheriffs, 111
pardoned, 117
sentenced to death, 116
Cortez, Romaldo, 107–9, 116
cotton, 129, 131
Cotulla, 114
Council House fight, 31–34, 35–36, 40
cronyism, 125–26
Crum, Allen, 186–87
Cuba, 180
Culbertson, Charles, 48
Curry, Jesse, 173

D

Dallas, TX, 134, 135, 136, 171–82
Davis, Edmund J., 53–55, 94
Day, Larry, 186–87
de Chenar, Coleman, 190
Democratic party, 140, 143–49
divorce, 48
Douglas, Kelsey, 35
Duderstadt, Fred, 92, 93
Duke of Duval, 140–50
Duval county, 140–50
Dwyer, Joseph E., 58–59

E

Eagle's Nest, 44
education, Texan, 39

elections of 1948, 143–49
embezzlement, 99–102

F

Facts Forum, 136
Fannin, James W., 19, 21
feminists, 71
Ferguson, James Edward, 119–
22, 124–25, 127, 128
Ferguson, Miriam Amanda
"Ma," 119–28
accomplishments, 127–28
cronyism, 125–26
death of, 128
early life, 119
elected governor, 123
and Ku Klux Klan, 124
as Lyndon Johnson
supporter, 127
pardons convicts, 124–
25, 127
second term, 126–27
First Amendment, 165
Fisher, John King, 61
Flynt, Larry, 166
forgery, 29
Fort Worth, 180
fraud, election, 143–49
Frazier, Buell Wesley, 180
Freethought Society, 161
fugitive, 87, 91–92, 107–18
Fults, Ralph, 153, 157–58

G

Galveston, TX, 2–6
gambling, 131
Glover, Robert M., 110–11
González, Jesús, 115

governor, woman, 119–28
Grass Fight, 18
Gray, F. B., 100–101
Great Raid of 1840, 36

H

Ham, Cephas K., 17
Hamer, Frank A., 156–57, 159
Hamilton, Raymond, 156
Hardin, John Wesley, 85–95
becomes lawyer, 95
captured, 94
as cowboy, 92–93
death of, 95
as fugitive, 87, 91–92
marriage, 93–94
as murderer, 85–86, 88, 89,
90, 91
in prison, 94–95
pursued by Texas Rangers,
90–91
Heatly, Maurice Dean, 189–90
Helms, Jack, 94
Henry, O. (William Sidney
Porter), 96–106
accused of embezzlement,
99–102
as bank teller, 98–99
death of, 104
early life, 96
marriage, 98
as newspaper columnist, 99
in prison, 103
pseudonym, 103–4
stories, 102–103, 103,
104–6
Hickok, "Wild Bill," 93
Hidell, Alek James, 177–78

Hinton, Ted, 158–59, 160
House Un-American Activities
    Committee, 164
Houston, Sam, 11, 19, 21, 22,
    23–24, 25–27, 34
    as president of Texas
        republic, 39–40
    sympathy for Indians, 38,
        39–40
Houston, TX, 134, 135
Hunt, H. L., 129–39
    as critic of J. F.
        Kennedy, 136
    death of, 136
    early life, 132
    as father, 133–34
    as gambler, 131
    marriages, 134–36, 137–38
    net worth, 129
    nicknames, 131–32
    as oil and real estate
        speculator, 131
    as publication founder,
        136–37
    secret personal life, 137–38

I
"Indian problem," 34

J
Jackson, Andrew, 1, 10
James, Jesse, 66
Johnson, Lyndon Baines, 127,
    140, 143–49, 173, 175
Johnston, Albert Sidney, 32
Joiner, Columbus M. "Dad," 133
Jones, W. D., 153–56
judge, 41–50

July, Jim, 68
justice of the peace, 41, 44, 48

K
Kearney, Larry, 6
Kenedy, TX, 107
Kennedy, Jacqueline, 174
Kennedy, John F., 171–82
    assassination, 136–37
Kerpelman, Leonard, 161
kidnappings, 154, 168–69
killing spree, 183–92
knife fighter, 15
Ku Klux Klan, 89, 123, 124

L
Lafitte, Jean, 1–10, 13
    abandons Galveston, 6
    allegiance to Mexico, 2
    death of, 6, 7
    early life, 4–5
    and Galveston, 2–4
    legends about, 3, 7
    marriage, 8
    as murderer, 8–9
    pardoned by Madison, 1
    and slave trade, 5
Lafitte, Pierre, 1, 4
Lallemand, Charles Françoise
    Antoine, 9–10
Lamar, Mirabeau B., 29, 31–40
    death of, 39
    dreams of Texas empire,
        37–38
    feelings about Indians, 38
    loses supporters, 38–39
    support of education in
        Texas, 39

land speculation, 14, 15–16, 18
Langtry, Lillie, 44–45
Langtry, TX, 44
Laredo, TX, 113
Las Cuevas War, 59–61
Lavergne, Gary, 192
Leissner, Kathy, 188
Levine, Christina, 8
Life Line, 136–37
Lockhart, Matilda, 31, 36
Long, James, 3, 13
Louisiana, 1, 13–14

M
madam, 21–30
manhunt, 107–18
Mann, Pamelia, 21–30
    death of, 29
    marriages, 23–24
    as proprietor of Mansion
        House, 27–29
    run-ins with law, 28–29
    and Sam Houston, 25–27
Martinez, Ramiro (Ray), 186–
    87
mass murder, 183–92
Masterson, Bat, 49
Matson, Carey Cheek, 53
Maverick, Mary, 31, 33
McCoy, Houston, 186–87
McLeod, Hugh, 34
McNelly, Leander, 51–61
    and cattle thieves, 59–61
    as Civil War hero, 51–52
    death of, 61
    and lawlessness at
        Mexican border, 56,
        57–58

marriage, 53
    as spy, 51, 56–57
    in State Police, 54
    as Texas Ranger, 55–61
Methvin, Henry, 156–57
Mexican Americans, 140, 142
Mexico, 1, 2–4, 15, 163–64
    lawlessness at border with
        U.S., 56, 57–58
    and Texas independence,
        19, 27
Morris, W. T. "Brack," 107–
    8, 110
Muguara, Chief, 31–32, 40
murders, 8–9, 14–15, 47, 85–86,
    88, 89, 90, 91, 153, 169
Murphy, Jim, 79–81, 82–83
Murray, Bill, 161, 163, 168–69,
    169–70
Murray, Garth, 169
Murray v. Curlett, 161

N
Navasota, TX, 22
Neill, James C., 11, 19–20
New Orleans, Battle of, 1
Nichols, James, 36–37
Nueces Strip, 56
Number Thirteen, 2

O
O'Hair, Jon Garth, 161, 163,
    165, 166, 169
O'Hair, Madalyn Murray,
    161–70
    arrested, 161
    deported from Mexico,
        163–64

early life, 169
founds American Atheists,
164–65
kidnapped, 168–69
marriage, 164, 169
murdered, 169
as speech writer, 166
and Susan Abramovitz,
161, 163
O'Hair, Richard, 164
oil tycoon, 129–39
Old Casuse, 57, 60
Ord, Edward O., 56–57
Oswald, Lee Harvey, 136,
171–82
attempts suicide, 179
attempts to assassinate
Edwin Walker, 178
early life, 178–80
hatred for America, 181
and Kennedy
assassination, 172–75
murdered, 171
tries to go to Cuba and the
Soviet Union, 180
Oswald, Marguerite, 177
Oswald, Marina, 177, 180
outlaws, 151–60

P

Paramore, Green, 94
pardons, 124–25, 127
Parker, Bonnie, 151–160. *See
also* Barrow, Clyde
captured and killed, 157
devotion to Clyde
Barrow, 158
early life, 151–52

films about, 160
as kidnapper, 154
as poet, 154, 158, 160
as robber, 154–55
Parr, Archie, 140, 142
Parr, George B., 140–50
amasses fortune, 142
commits suicide, 150
convicted of income tax
evasion, 142
declares bankruptcy, 149
elections of 1948, 143–49
pardoned by Truman,
142–43
Peak, Junius "June," 79
Peddy, George, 143
Phil Donahue (tv show), 165
pirate, 1–10
Plum Creek, Battle of, 36–37
poachers, 42
political activism, 161–70
poll tax, 144
Poor Richard's Universal Life
Church, 166
Porter, William Sidney. *See*
Henry, O.
Potter, Joseph H., 60–61
prayer in schools, 161
privateers, 1–10
Prohibition, 127
prostitute, 90
public school system, 39

R

Ray, Ruth, 136, 139
Reed, Jim, 64–65
Rice, Elizabeth and Eleanor, 24
Roach, Athol Estes, 98, 99

robberies, 17–18, 75–78, 154–55
Robertson, Felix, 123
Robertson, Sterling C., 23
Robin Hood, Texan, 72–84
Robledo, Martín, 110–11
Rohrer, Conrad, 25, 26, 27
Roman Catholic religion, 15
Roths, John Henry, 169
Ruby, Jack, 136–37, 171, 175, 182
Runaway Scrape, 22
Rusk, Thomas J., 27

S

Salas, Luis, 145–46
saloons, 43–44
San Antonio, TX, 11, 16–17, 19, 31, 41, 43, 161
Sandbar Fight, 14–15
Sandoval, Jesús, 57
San Saba Mine, 16–17
Santa Anna, Antonio López de, 11, 19, 21, 27
Schnabel, Henry, 110–11
school prayer, 161
Selman, John, 95
separation of church and state, 165
silver, 16–17
slavery, 5, 13–14
Smithwick, Noah, 21–22, 37, 40
smuggler, 1–10
sniper, 183–192
Society of Separationists, 165
Soviet Union, 179, 180
Spain, 1–4, 9–10
Sparks, S. F., 26

spies, 1, 9–10, 51, 56–57, 70
Starr, Belle, 62–71
    arrested, 67
    charged with horse
        theft, 68
    as Civil War spy, 70
    as deadly shot, 67–68
    death of, 68
    early life, 62, 64
    friendships with outlaws,
        65–66
    legends about, 69–71
    lovers, 64
    marriage, 64, 66, 68
Starr, Sam, 66
State Police (Texas), 54, 94
Sterling, Ross, 126
Stevenson, Coke, 143–49
Sutton-Taylor feud, 55, 94

T

Taylor, John, 94
Texas
    annexation of, 37–38
    education, 39
    independence, 3, 19, 27
Texas Rangers, 15, 36–37, 44,
    45, 51–61, 55–61
    pursue John Hardin, 90–91
    pursue Sam Bass, 78–79,
        81–82
Texas School Book Depository,
    174–75, 176–77, 180
Thornton, Roy, 153
Tippit, J. D., 174–75
Toliver, Beatrice, 7–8
Travis, William Barrett, 18, 20

truce, 34, 36
Truman, Harry, 143
Tye, Frania, 134–35, 137–38
Tyler, TX, 134

U
ultraconservatism, 136
University of Texas, 121,
  183–92

V
Veramendi, Maria Ursula de, 16
Vinegaroon, 43–44

W
Walker, Edwin, 178
War of 1812, 1, 2, 13
Warren Commission, 171, 175–
  76, 180–81
Waters, David, 166–68
wealth, 129
Webb, Charles, 94
Webster, Booker, 34

Whitman, Charles, 183–92
  court martialed, 189
  early life, 187–89
  killed, 187
  kills mother, 187, 191
  kills wife, 187, 190–91
  in Marines, 188
  marriage, 188
  mood swings, 189
women
  bandit, 62–71
  brothel owner, 21–30
  governor, 119–28
  most hated in America,
    161–70
  outlaw, 151–60
Wright, Norris, 14–15
writer, 96–106

Y
Yarborough, Ralph, 173
Yoakum, Henderson K., 21
Younger, Bruce, 66

About the Author

As a native Texan, storyteller and author Donna Ingham has long been fascinated by the history of the Lone Star State and by some of its more notorious characters. A former college English professor, she thrives on doing research and writing it into some kind of coherent form as she has in collections such as *Mysteries and Legends of Texas* and three earlier books for Globe Pequot Press. When she is not holed up in her study writing, she is out on the road as a touring professional storyteller. Ingham lives in Spicewood, Texas, with her husband, Jerry.